# A Welshman in
## Garfield Owen – Rugby

# Andrew Hardcastle

## London League Publications Ltd

**A Welshman in Halifax**
**Garfield Owen – Rugby footballer**
© Andrew Hardcastle. Foreword © Robert Gate.

The moral right of Andrew Hardcastle to be identified as the author has been asserted.

Cover design © Stephen McCarthy.

Front cover: Garfield takes on the Leeds defence at Thrum Hall, supported by Keith Williams, (Photo courtesy *Halifax Courier*); inset photo: Garfield wearing his Welsh Rugby Union international shirt and cap. Back cover: Tackling try–scoring ace Brian Bevan.

All photographs in this book are from private collections unless otherwise credited. No copyright has been intentionally breached; please contact London League Publications Ltd if you believe there has been a breach of copyright.

A CIP catalogue record for this book is available from the British Library.

First published in Great Britain in May 2011 by:
London League Publications Ltd, P.O. Box 65784, London NW2 9NS

ISBN:                            978-1903659-55-7

Cover design by:          Stephen McCarthy Graphic Design
                                   46, Clarence Road, London N15 5BB

Layout:                        Peter Lush

Printed and bound in Great Britain by:
CPI Antony Rowe, Chippenham and Eastbourne

Garfield Owen wishes to dedicate this book to his parents, his wonderful wife Marlene who has been a constant support in their lives together, and to Russell and Sally, their now grown up children and their families who have been a source of great pride and joy.

Garfield Owen's share of the profits from the book will be given to Parkinson's UK Halifax branch.

# Foreword

Sometimes you hear someone say that it is not always wise to meet your heroes, especially those of your childhood. They say you might be disappointed; you might not like them; they might have feet of clay. Trust me, Garfield Owen does not disappoint in any way. As a boy I did indeed hero-worship Garfield. As far as I was concerned he was perfect, the king of the castle that was Thrum Hall. His turning professional in 1956 coincided with my newly found infatuation with rugby league. That infatuation with the game has undoubtedly waned but my admiration for Garfield Owen has never diminished.

In later life I had cause to write about Garfield as a rugby player and that brought me into direct contact with him. I helped him occasionally and he helped me. As a multi-talented sportsman he was a paragon, a genuine role model. As a man he is affable, courteous, humorous and modest. Latterly his work for Parkinson's UK has highlighted his humanitarian qualities. All-in-all, if ever there was a good egg it's got to be Garfield.

As for feet of clay - no way. More like feet of cast iron, feet of thunder, educated feet, feet to die for. As a rugby full-back in both codes Garfield was a veritable virtuoso. He had a superabundance of the qualities a full-back of his era needed, many of which unfortunately now appear much less relevant, particularly in rugby league. It is difficult to imagine how anyone could kick, catch and tackle as well as Garfield. To modern followers of the game it is equally difficult to explain how vitally important goal-kicking was in the 1950s and 1960s. Unlike today, when there is always likely to be yet another try along in the next few minutes, goal-kicking was of paramount importance, particularly in big games when try-scoring might be minimal. Garfield was worth his weight in gold in such matches because the halfway line was no barrier to men like him.

Kickers such as Jimmy Ledgard, Bernard Ganley, Lewis Jones, Johnny Wilson, Fred Griffiths, Cyril Kellett, Don and Neil Fox, to name but a few, were always game to attempt seemingly impossible long-range penalties, the sort that no modern kicker would even contemplate. Garfield was top of the range in that sphere. Not only was he capable of superlative goal-kicking, he was consistently capable of it. In almost 300 first class games he failed to kick a goal in only 17, a truly phenomenal performance, especially when it is remembered that he played in teams that were not particularly successful.

Apart from his deadly marksmanship, Garfield's field kicking and touch kicking gained miles of territory for his sides. Consequently, newspaper previews of Halifax or Keighley matches often carried warnings from opposition coaches and captains stressing the absolute necessity of not giving away penalties, because of the damage Owen might wreak. His fielding of the ball was nigh on miraculous and rendered all the more effective because he positioned himself so well – almost as if he knew just how far and to where opposing kickers would propel the ball. Under the laws of the game in Garfield's days, the ball was not deemed to have gone out of play until it hit the ground over the touch-line and, with kickers desperate to make as much ground as possible with penalties to touch, Garfield was in his element. His own touch-finders were invariably enormous, while he had the ability and judgement to pull balls out of touch before they hit the ground, which sometimes beggared belief. If he was playing today the legislators would have to alter the 40-20 law to give everyone else a chance.

And what about Garfield's tackling? Well, it was a thing of beauty, clean, low, thrilling, memorable. Of course, he must have missed some tackles, but they are hard to recall. Even harder to recall are any form of misdemeanours committed by Garfield. With talents such as his, his actions spoke for him. I never saw him commit a remotely low act on the pitch, nor do I think anyone else ever did.

Andrew Hardcastle has done the game a wonderful service in presenting this biography of a good man and a sublime player. Feet of clay? Pull the other one!

**Robert Gate**
**February 2011**

Robert Gate is a lifelong Halifax supporter and prolific writer on the history of rugby league. His many works include the two volumes of *Gone North*, about Welsh rugby union players who switched codes to play rugby league.

Garfield's parents, Jim and Blodwen Owen.

# Preface

At a recent charity dinner I was introduced by the master of ceremonies as the only Welshman he knew who was named after an Irish punt, the Garryowen. Of course this is not true. I did though have a sporting career punctuated by moments of sheer luck, some of it like this connected with my name. As I look back I must have had more than my fair share.

My parents certainly were among the most tolerant of people, allowing me to do more or less what I wanted. I lived the life of Riley. Staying at school until the age of 19 was practically unheard of in those days, especially when I made little or no contribution to the household finances. Indeed I was the parasitic cuckoo in the nest. I did it my way and took great liberties. Never ever did I hear any swear words, and they were never demonstrative in their feelings towards me. Oh, how I wish I could turn back the clock and show my appreciation.

Schooldays proved to be marvellous. I did just enough to keep myself out of trouble. But one day Idwal Rees, the headmaster, was watching the school team play rugby union for a while and then disappeared. Afterwards, there was a message on my desk to "see me in my office". Immediately after break time I arrived there wondering what I had done. When he got up he opened a cabinet and there they were, a brand spanking new pair of Cotton Oxford boots, size 9, all gleaming and bright. "Take these", he said. "We can't have you running around with bandages holding your boots together." I honestly believe that they were a new pair he had ordered for himself! Talk about looking a gift horse in the mouth. What an understanding headmaster.

As well as the Irish punt, my name also led to a unique relationship developing between the Garryowen Football Club and myself. I had been basking in the reflected glory of the famous Irish club for many years, but despite my explaining to everyone that I was not the person who introduced the Garryowen or "up-and-under", rugby correspondents, who should have known better, continued to ignore my protests and even started to call me a legend in my own lifetime! This was further consolidated by the dulcet tones of Eddie Waring when I signed for Halifax. In the end I decided to give up denying it and just enjoy the confusion.

The myth continued until an article on the Garryowen club's centenary appeared in the *Sunday Observer* in 1984, with the explanation that the name in Gaelic meant Owen's Garden, and a quote from the New Zealand rugby historian Wallace Reyburn, who had written asking the question, "Who was this Welshman, Garry Owen, you've named the up-and-under after?" It was time to put the matter straight once and for all. I wrote to the Garryowen club's president, Morgan Costelloe, telling him that I was the Welshman who had traded upon his club's legendary play. However, no damage had been done and showing typical Irish generosity he sent me a centenary tie.

I wish to thank Andrew Hardcastle for his unstinting patience and attention to detail in researching reference books. Without his enthusiasm this book would never have been produced. I hope his probing has revealed the good and the bad in my character, always being aware of course, that not to take advantage of the presence of luck would have been foolish.

Sport has given me a good life, but I wonder has sport done well by me? I would like to leave the last words to my two granddaughters, which put me firmly back in my place. Sarah, then three years old, looked up at a photograph of me in my Welsh jersey and cap and asked my daughter-in-law: "Mummy, why is grandpa wearing that silly hat?" And Eleanor, aged 10, returned from a school trip to North Wales to tell Marlene my wife: "I thought you said grandpa was famous. I asked everybody I met and none of them knew him. I even asked the bus driver and he'd never heard of him either..."

**Garfield Owen**
**Halifax, January 2011.**

## About the author

Andrew Hardcastle is a retired schoolteacher, married with two grown-up children. He played rugby union at school and college, but grew up with rugby league, both amateur and professional. He became connected with Halifax RLFC, where he has been club historian for 30 years, timekeeper and one-time occasional second team player. He has contributed to a variety of publications, magazines and newspapers, writing mostly on rugby league.

His previous books have been:
*The Thrum Hall Story, a history of Halifax RLFC,* 1986.
*They played for Halifax,* 1987
*Halifax at Wembley,* 1987.
*Thrum Hall Greats,* 1994.
*Halifax Rugby League, The First Hundred Years,* Tempus, 1998.
*Lost, the former cricket clubs and grounds of Halifax and Calderdale,* Cricket Heritage Project, 2006.

# Introduction

Some time in 1965 or 1966 I was playing rugby with a group of mates on a patch of grass below West View Park in Halifax - we did most evenings. We played the proper rugby league rules, which still allowed unlimited tackles, so we didn't kick much, but on this occasion the ball found itself in Warley Road, which ran alongside the park, and it cannoned into a passing car. The car screeched to a halt and its driver marched towards us. "Keep your ball under control," he remonstrated. "You're lucky I don't kick it out of the park!" And off he went.

"Who's he think he is, Ronnie James?" asked one of my mates, as soon as the driver was safely out of earshot. It made the rest of us smile, because we had recognised him as Garfield Owen, who we had seen playing for Keighley and knew was a former Halifax player from the days before we started watching. He could probably have kicked the ball much further than our current hero Ronnie James.

What we were unaware of at the time was just how good a kicker and player he really was – good enough to play international rugby union for Wales six times in succession, to have his signing as a professional with Halifax screened live on national television on our favourite programme *Sportsview*, and to smash goal-kicking records at both rugby league clubs he represented. He wasn't just a player, he was a superstar.

Later in life I came to know him quite well when we were both committee members of the Halifax Rugby League Past Players' Association. A gentleman in every sense of the word, he was and still is a well-liked figure with everyone. It was a great honour when he recently suggested that we try to put together this book.

He is a modest man. Throughout the book's preparation he often found it hard to talk about himself – he had experienced such relative success that he felt it was boastful. He told the story that as a student he had a desire to do something different and hit on the idea of reading the entire Bible. He only ever got as far as Exodus, but on the night before his first Welsh trial opened the book at random rather than the place where he had left his bookmark, and his eyes alighted on Proverbs 27, which begins:
"Boast not thyself of tomorrow;
For thou knowest not what a day may bring forth.
Let another man praise thee, and not thine own mouth;
A stranger, and not thine own lips."

He tried to live by it, but admits that he has failed miserably, either when people have got things wrong about him, or shown a general interest and asked about his career. The sections of the book which sing his praises are always my words, or quotations from journalists or other authors, never his own.

His story is one of remarkable success in many different sports and walks of life, successes that were beyond his wildest dreams in his boyhood days in the small Welsh village of Llanharan.

**Andrew Hardcastle**
**Halifax**
**February 2011**

## Acknowledgements

The book was fashioned around a series of interviews at Garfield's home. He and Marlene were always the most hospitable of hosts; I owe them grateful thanks for making this part of the process so easy and enjoyable.

As Halifax Rugby League Club historian, facts and figures relating to Halifax were all to hand, but for Garfield's career outside the club, I am indebted to many individuals for their invaluable help. Mike Dams provided a tremendous amount of help on Newport Rugby Union Club, and Wales in general, and was always quick to answer my queries. At Keighley, John Pitchford and Ann Self were really supportive, they too going out of their way to provide the information I sought. Mike and John were kind enough to read the chapters on their clubs, ensuring I wasn't totally biased towards Halifax.

Statistical details compiled by the Rugby League Record Keepers Club, printed in their Teams and Scorers booklets and History of Rugby League series, were invaluable, as were historical price conversion and other websites for background information.

Garfield kept a scrapbook of press cuttings and photographs, so national newspaper reports were readily available, though sometimes the name of the journalist or even his newspaper was unfortunately missing. Stephen Bennett of Newport was good enough to send excerpts from press reports in the *South Wales Argus* of all Garfield's matches with Wales and Newport. Libraries at Halifax, Keighley and Leeds provided easy access to microfilm back numbers of the *Halifax Courier*, *Keighley News* and *Yorkshire Post*, while the Rugby League archive at the University of Huddersfield gave access to RFL minute books – my thanks to Sarah Wickham.

Four journalists between them probably saw just about every senior game Garfield played – Jack Davis of the *South Wales Echo*, Frank Williams and Roland Tinker of the *Halifax Courier*, and Eric Lund of the *Keighley News*. Their views are quoted extensively.

Club records at Llanharan, Maesteg, Wrexham and Old Crossleyans were harder to find, lost in fires and other catastrophes over the years.

But Harry Wolstenholme and Paul Jackson at Crossleyans, Keith Taylor and Hugh Smith at Llanharan, Dennis Thomas at Maesteg and the Webmaster at Wrexham all helped as much as they could. Fellow Rugby League historians Tony Collins, Graham Morris, Alex Service, Michael Latham, Mike Turner, and Mike Rylance were their usual efficient selves in providing additional information. Gerry Wright, Gordon Priestley and David Thorpe are others to whom I owe thanks.

Several of Garfield's acquaintances and former playing colleagues were happy to provide memories, including Adrian Trotman, Eddie Deasey, Ronnie James, Johnny Freeman, Jack Scroby and Ken Dean.

Thanks also to Robert Gate, who checked my factual accuracy and provided a perceptive and knowledgeable foreword to complement the book.

The photographs mostly came from Garfield's own collection, and some from mine. Mike Astin provided a great service by reproducing those stuck into the scrapbook. David Hanson at the *Halifax Courier* was as helpful as ever, and my thanks go to the *Courier* for allowing the use of photographs which are theirs. Several other photos have no indication of who took them, but no copyright has been intentionally breached.

**Andrew Hardcastle**
**February 2011**

London League Publications Ltd would like to thanks Michael O'Hare for sub-editing the book, Steve McCarthy for designing the cover and the staff of CPI Antony Rowe Ltd for printing it.

**Peter Lush & Dave Farrar**
**April 2011**

# Bibliography

## Biographies and autobiographies
Jonathan Davies with Peter Corrigan, *Jonathan An Autobiography*, Stanley Paul 1989

Gareth Edwards, *Rugby*, Partridge Press 1986

Simon Foster, Robert Gate & Peter Lush, *Trevor Foster, The Life of a Rugby League Legend*, London League Publications 2005

Scott Gibbs, *Getting Physical, The Autobiography of Scott Gibbs*, Ebury Press 2000

Lewis Jones, *King of Rugger*, Stanley Paul 1958

Cliff Morgan with Geoffrey Nicholson, *Cliff Morgan: The Autobiography – Beyond the Fields of Play*, Hodder & Stoughton 1996

Gus Risman, *Rugby Renegade*, Stanley Paul 1958

David Watkins & Brian Dobbs, *The Dave Watkins Story*, Pelham 1971

## Other books
Maurice Bamford, *The Second Half, More Funny Stories in Rugby League*, Vertical Editions 2007

Robert Gate, *Gone North Volume 2*, 1988

W.J. Hicks (Ed.), *Boys' Book of All Sport*, News Chronicle 1955 and other years

Derek Hirst, *Halifax Bradley Hall Gold Club, A Century of Golf 1907-2007*, Bradley Hall 2007

Robert Light (Ed.), *No Sand Dunes in Featherstone*, London League Publications 2010

H. Ludlam, *The History of Rishworth School*, 1973

Graham Williams, Peter Lush & Dave Farrar, *The British Rugby League Records Book*, London League Publications, 2009

T.J. Witts, *The Forgotten Years, A History of Llanharan & District*, 1975

## Reference books
Terry Godwin, *The International Rugby Championship 1883–1983*, Willow Books 1984

John Griffiths, *The Phoenix Book of International Rugby Records*, Dent & Sons 1987

Steve Lewis & John Griffiths, *The Essential History of Rugby Union – Wales*, Headline Book Publishing 2003

## Booklets and brochures
Trevor Delaney, Clive Harrison, John Pitchford & Ann Self, *Lawkholme Lane, 100 years of Rugby 1885–1985*, Keighley RL Supporters Club 1985

Clive Harrison, John Pitchford & Ann Self, *A Lawkholme Gallery*, Keighley Rugby League Supporters Club 1987

## Other sources
Halifax Rugby League Club minute books

*The Rugby League Gazette*

Contemporary matchday programmes

# Contents

Hon. Treasurer:
P. Pratt
196 Ballinacurra Gardens,
Limerick
Tel: 28963 (H)
315233 (O)

Hon. Secretary:
O. M. Griffin,
36 Park Gardens,
Corbally,
Limerick
Tel. 43820 (H)
45152 (O)

Hon. Fixtures Secretary:
Billy Purcell,
27 Fortfield,
Raheen,
Limerick.
Tel. (061) 28828 (H)
316411 (O)

Mr. Garfield Owen,

8th October, 1984.

Many thanks for your recent kind letter on the occasion of our Centenary Year. It was great to hear from a "Garryowen Man", if I remember correctly, one who was well able to deal with any ball put up to him. Incidentally, we had Cardiff R.F.C. over last week end playing on our Centenary Match. They won, 13.6. Both Jack Mathews and Stan Bowes asked particularly to be remembered to you.

As a small token of appreciation I enclose a Garryowen Centenary tie.

Best wishes in Rugby,

Morgan Costelloe, President.

A letter to Garfield from the Garryowen Football Club in Ireland.

# 1. Growing up in Llanharan

The BBC cameras rolled as Garfield Owen sat nervously beside rugby league journalist Eddie Waring and Halifax Rugby League Club secretary Bill Hughes. It was Wednesday 17 October 1956, the *Sportsview* television programme was in full swing. The Welsh rugby union international full-back had agreed to turn professional with rugby league club Halifax, and it was national news.

Eddie had primed him with the questions for the interview so he could prepare his answers, only to throw him completely by asking the third question first, but he did manage to get his key message across. "This is the ideal time to safeguard my future," he told the viewers. Bill Hughes added that Halifax were paying "a substantial fee for the best full-back in the four countries". The cameras moved back to Peter Dimmock for the rest of the programme, leaving Garfield to set out on a new life in the north of England.

It was 24 years since he was born in Llanharan, a small village in South Wales between Bridgend and Cardiff, much like many other neighbouring villages. Once agricultural, by the 1930s it had changed into a mining community, several coal and tin mines in the area providing jobs for local people. Two of the village's residents were Jim Owen and Blodwen Mary Rees.

Jim was a coalminer at Llanharan Colliery and former star of the local rugby union team, which he had captained in 1927. Blodwen was a widow with three children: Margaret, Gwyneth and Ivor. They met when Jim, injured in a mining accident, had taken on a temporary job collecting insurance. Blodwen was on his round. She was impressed with Jim's sincerity and responsible attitude, his desire to take on a ready-made family at a difficult time making for a perfect partnership. They married in 1931 and became parents of a son, Garfield David Owen, on 20 March 1932. After Garfield, two more daughters, Avril and Marion, followed some years later. Together they lived on a long row of terraced houses on Bridgend Road in Llanharan.

These were the years of the Great Depression, with cuts in public spending and wages; income tax increased to 25 percent, high unemployment and widespread poverty. Times were tough, but Garfield hardly ever noticed. For him, an attraction in the village quickly became the sports ground, which housed Llanharan's rugby, cricket, tennis and bowls teams. Without television, computer games and other modern paraphernalia, it was how boys often spent their time. Pinching a rugby ball to kick around at half-time on Saturday afternoons became a delight as Garfield and his mates, unable to afford individual sports equipment like tennis rackets, took to team

1

games where a football or cricket ball could serve 20 or more. The sight of scrumptious cream cornets prepared for the cricketers' teas was an added incentive to become members of the cricket team when they were old enough.

A clubhouse was being built at the time to replace the primitive construction that preceded it. Many of the villagers mucked in, but Garfield preferred to find a ball to play with.

Sport played a big part in village life, for some even providing a way out of their economic difficulties. Local rugby union star Danny Pascoe had won international honours with Wales in 1923, then cashed in on his talents by turning to rugby league with Leeds, York and Keighley. Another Llanharan boy, Eynon Hawkins, also made a name for himself in both rugby codes, playing six times for the Welsh rugby league international team between 1949 and 1953.

Away from rugby, there were opportunities in boxing. Llanharan might only have been a small village, but it had recently produced top boxers in Charlie Bundy, Ron Pritchard and Sid Worgan. Charlie Bundy fought Tommy Farr for the Welsh heavyweight title three times during the 1930s, but lost narrowly on points every time, as he did to Bruce Woodcock, who was later to challenge for the world title. His last fight was at Llanharan Welfare Ground in 1942 when he beat Scottish champion Wally Bridgmond. Ron Pritchard, chief sparring partner of Welsh bantam champion Norman Lewis, fought 170 bouts in a career that ended in 1951. Sid Worgan went even further, winning the Welsh title in 1944.

Garfield watched these great fighters train in the gymnasium by the High Corner House pub, but did not fancy taking up boxing himself. More in his line was athletics, another sport in which Llanharan could boast local heroes. The up-and-coming Hywel Williams was to win the Welsh and later British decathlon titles in the 1950s, before competing in the Commonwealth Games in 1958.

In the more sedate realms of snooker, Gwyn Howells, a friend of his father, had won the Welsh championship in 1937. Garfield was soon to take to snooker and billiards himself, notching century breaks by the time he was 15 and being chosen as an opponent of multiple world champion Joe Davis in an exhibition match.

Rugby was the most prominent sport, the local rugby union team having been formed in the 1890s by boys from the nearby Cowbridge Grammar School and the sons of the local squire, the Blandy-Jenkins family who lived in Llanharan House. Garfield's next door neighbour, Adrian Trotman, a few years older than Garfield, became a player there before moving on to Swansea and Neath after winning Welsh University honours. While Trotman was a schoolteacher, most of the other players had connections with the local collieries, which brought rugby men to the village. The club thrived, continuing to play through the years of the Second World War, 1939 to 1945, which took up most of Garfield's youthful days. His father volunteered for evening duty with the Home Guard after his shift at the colliery, for there was always the possibility of a stray bomb, dropped by the German Luftwaffe searching for the arsenal at Bridgend. Garfield knew all about the arsenal, because his mother worked there making shells. Each day in summer it also impinged on his fun.

There was lots of time for fun, which more often than not meant sport. During the war years Britain operated a system of double summer time, the clocks moving forward a further hour, meaning long light evenings. Rugby was set aside so that Garfield and his mates, budding Glamorgan county cricketers in their minds, could play their summer game across the main road, then largely devoid of traffic, chalking wickets on a lamp-post. And each morning they had to halt play for 10 minutes while the buses thundered past, carrying his mother and what seemed like all the other women of the area to Bridgend – then another 10 minutes as they thundered back in the evening. Worse for Garfield was that these were years of sweet-rationing, which fell to as low as eight ounces a month, and continued well beyond the end of the war. Not only that, prices nearly doubled, so it was not always possible to even buy up to the limit.

His parents provided a wonderful upbringing, spoiling him to some extent. His father would put his wage packet on the table, and from there his mother took over and ran the household. It must have been a struggle for her in particular to bring up six children, and Garfield regrets, in hindsight, that he did not appreciate either of them more. He remembers coming home one night wanting toast, but the fire had been built up with small coal in preparation for damping down for the next morning, so could not be used for toasting. His mother got the bread and went next door to toast it there, only on her return for Garfield to say he didn't want it anymore; his father was furious, yet never once did he hear him swear.

Money was tight and the penny or tuppence change when he was sent on errands would have been important to his mother, but he had no qualms about spending it at the billiard hall. If he did not get his own way, or if he was told off, he would think that he was being put on and contemplate running away.

The errands were to the local shops, including butcher Mr Freeman's, around 80 yards down Bridgend Road. He had his own abattoir at the back, which did little to improve the smell of the street. At the grocer's, the Owens, like most other residents, were allowed credit. On one occasion Garfield was sent there for the shopping only to find a stand-in assistant who looked at their account, saw the growing bill, and sent him home to tell his mother there would be no more goods until it was settled. She was irate, more in embarrassment at who in such a smallish village might have overheard the grocer, and marched up there herself to sort the matter out.

Sometimes Garfield did manage to show some appreciation. At Christmas he and his step-brother Ivor visited the grocer's to find out the bill and clubbed together to pay it, so when she called herself there was a pleasant surprise.

Dolau Elementary School brought out a love of drawing and art, and provided more opportunities for sport, rugby in the winter and cricket in the summer, though there were no school teams. It also gave him a good  enough education to pass the entrance examination in 1943 for Cowbridge Grammar School, around five miles away, reached at first by bus or when in the sixth form by bicycle.

During the war years it was under the temporary headship of a strict disciplinarian with the same surname as him, Owen. All the teachers were known as masters. "We were respectful," he says. "We raised our caps not just to the masters at school, but to policemen and doctors." Cowbridge was just the place for Garfield – a school renowned for sport and rugby in particular. In the first games lesson Mr Hughes, who taught Welsh as well as PE, lined the boys up and allocated them a position according to their size and appearance. "You're a hooker," he said when he saw Garfield, and that was where he played that morning. He finished the lesson with a ripped shirt, which did not please his mother when he got home, for vital but sparse clothing coupons were needed to buy a new one. She told him to find a different position, so he settled on full-back. It was a good choice because he was soon playing there in organised sport for the first time in the Cowbridge junior rugby union team, the under-14s.

The school's pre-war headmaster returned from war service in 1945. He was a rugby man called Idwal Rees. He was no ordinary rugby man either, for he had played 14 times for Wales in the 1930s, on three occasions as centre partner to winger Arthur Bassett, who had signed for Halifax Rugby League Club in 1939. Mr Rees, captain in some of his international appearances, was able to provide inspiration for young Garfield as he moved up his school, as by then he was showing his skills as a goalkicking full-back of real talent in the school team. Often for home matches Mr Rees would be the referee. Garfield remembers him as something of an asset: "'Whose ball is it?' we'd ask at the scrum. 'Ours!' he would reply."

It was the headmaster who provided him with his first decent pair of boots. His own were falling apart and held together with bandages, when Mr Rees secretly provided him with a pair of Cotton Oxfords, the best make around at the time. Garfield wore a size eight, but Mr Rees gave him size nine and told him to wear an extra pair of socks. He was ordered not to say a word to anyone, for as well as possible accusations of favouritism, there were also concerns around professionalism, as there often were in rugby union circles, and issues with clothing coupons, with restrictions on how they could be used.

By this time he was spending hours each day on individual practice, honing both his fitness and general sporting skills. He did not mind training on his own or with his step-brother, and would be up at 6.30am running down Bridgend Road and up to Llanharry and back, around three miles in total. Ivor was five years older, fast and strong, a fly-half or centre and eventually full-back in the school team. Sometimes a friend, Tony White, did the same training run, and Garfield would try to beat him, a task not much easier than it was against Ivor.

To help with the rugby he often tried wearing a boot only on his left foot, forcing him to kick with that, and making him almost as adept with it as his right. He practised catching the ball and returning kicks, his father sometimes shouting encouragement from the sidelines to "make an angle" – running back infield to allow a longer touch-finding kick.

Friends were roped in and asked to kick the ball over his head then try to beat him to it before he could turn and get back. With his goalkicking, he always favoured making a raised tee by digging into the ground with his heel, so that he could get his kicking foot properly under the ball as modern-day kickers do with an actual tee. This was only allowed with penalty kicks in rugby union at the time though, conversion attempts having to be made with another player known as a 'placer' lying on the ground with his finger holding the ball in position – annoying if he took his finger away too soon and the ball slipped over as it was about to be kicked; there was no replacing allowed with the opposition having started to charge towards the kicker.

Mr Rees helped too. Noting a few missed goalkicks in school matches, he advised that Garfield keep his head down: "The posts are not going to move. Don't lift your head until you hear the roar of the spectators. If there is no roar, the kick has missed and there is no point looking up anyway."

In his athletics training he became pals with decathlon starlet Hywel Williams, two years his senior. The two would train together on weights, really getting into it and developing their shoulder muscles to be able to throw fair distances. Throwing events became his preference, in particular the javelin, and while Garfield would never have been able to get one himself, Hywel managed to procure one from somewhere. However, travelling any distance with a 2.5 metre spear could be tricky, necessitating standing on the open platform at the back of the double-decker bus with the javelin outside.

It was a bus that almost caused his demise. Jumping off the platform once as it slowed, he raced across the road straight in front of an overtaking car being driven, he soon discovered, by the local Presbyterian Sunday School teacher. The car screeched to a halt in the nick of time, Garfield scurrying off into the billiard hall to escape. The driver knew where he had gone though, chasing after him to give him the biggest rollicking of his life.

Other out-of-school activities in these teenage years were with the Army Cadets, a local branch having been formed by Mr Stone, the father of one of the village boys, to help keep them out of mischief. With the war having just ended, anything that pertained to the army, air force or navy caught the imagination of youngsters, having more relevance than similar groups like Boy Scouts or the Boys' Brigade. Khaki uniforms were acquired, there was marching drill, and there were rugby, association football and cricket matches against other Army Cadet groups, where he met Arthur Morgan, who later became a Swansea Town (now City) and Plymouth Argyle footballer, and Brian Sparks, who was to feature many more times in his rugby career, both union and league. He and Brian won selection for the county Army Cadet XV, which played and won on the Llanharan ground. Lady Blandy-Jenkins came along to present the prizes, 10 Woodbines for each player, but two packets for Garfield who was the captain. The pair went on to play for Wales Army Cadets against England Cadets at Redruth in Cornwall.

School playing commitments on a Saturday meant there was rarely an opportunity to watch first-class rugby, and no television to see it on either. All the boys were aware of the Welsh international side though, back in action after the war, with heroes who they had never seen play, and most would probably have had dreams of turning out themselves at the national stadium, Cardiff Arms Park.

Garfield's heroes were Cardiff centre Bleddyn Williams and Newport's flying wingman Ken Jones, new young stars in a team that had shared the international championship in season 1946–47. There was never a chance to see them in action, but he did go along to an army international against New Zealand. He travelled on the service bus for his first sight of the Arms Park, an awe-inspiring sight, the singing of the national anthem blowing him away. The New Zealand Expeditionary Force, which had fought for the Allies during the war, had sent on tour a popular and skilful side known as the Kiwis, its stars soon afterwards to form the core of the All Blacks. What caught Garfield's imagination most in the match were the long, spiralling torpedo kicks of full-back Bob Scott. On his return home he begged his

6

parents for a new rugby ball for Christmas, and used it endlessly to perfect his own torpedo action. In his mind were thoughts that he could play every bit as well as the full-backs he had seen at the international.

By the late 1940s Garfield was becoming completely wrapped up in sport, which seemed to come so easily to him. Schoolwork was a lesser priority, though crucially he did enough to pass the School Certificate, the forerunner of 'O' Levels and GCSEs, which allowed him to stay on into the sixth form at Cowbridge. Most young lads in the village saw their futures down the pit, many of his age-group having already left school, the standard leaving age in these years being still just 14, but his growing love of sport gave him other ideas.

An austere economic climate under the post-war Labour government meant times could be just as hard as in the 1930s, and he considers himself really lucky that his parents put no pressure on him to leave school and find work. That was exactly the misfortune that had befallen his father, who in the 1920s had felt it necessary to give up the captaincy of Llanharan rugby club. As one of 12 children, the sooner he was concentrating on working the better.

With no such worries, Garfield's sporting prowess was able to blossom. He was made captain of the school's first XV in rugby and first XI in cricket in 1950. The chance of a unique treble with the captaincy of athletics, and the opportunity to become Head Boy, helped confirm his desire to say on for a third year in the sixth form, ostensibly to improve his qualifications, so that he was aged 19 by the time he finished school.

School cricket matches would generally be played with a composition cricket ball, which as a bowler Garfield could swing prodigiously. One school match saw him take 8 wickets for 2 runs. His bowling developed to such an extent that he won international selection for the Welsh Secondary Schools cricket team in successive years between 1948 and 1951. The third of these was played over two days at Old Trafford in Manchester on Thursday and Friday, 9 and 10 August, 1951. The England team included Peter Marner, who just 12 months later would become the youngest ever Lancashire County player, and prospective Yorkshire and England opening batsman Ken Taylor. Neither of those two succumbed to his bowling, but he remembers having Mike Barnard, later of Hampshire, caught in the slips in one of the earlier matches at Bournemouth. Another wicket came when he leapt to catch a lofted return drive, parried the ball and crashed into the umpire as he caught the falling ball low down. He also scored a few runs at Old Trafford as a lower order batsman, and was moved up the order in the second innings with Wales in search of quick runs, but perished early. The cricket bible *Wisden* included large sections on schools cricket, but only the public and independent schools; it completely neglected state schools, giving no facts and figures of these matches.

In athletics, his training with Hywel Williams came to fruition, reaching the very top for a schoolboy in 1949 when he was Glamorgan and Welsh Secondary Schools javelin champion. The *News Chronicle Boys Book of All Sports* the following year included a section, in among pictures of Stanley Matthews, Denis Compton and Ken Jones, of records supplied by the National Schools' Association. There in the Welsh secondary schools best performances list is the javelin record – G.D. Owen, Cowbridge Grammar School, 186 feet 6 inches, 1949. He had never thrown anything like that before, but one of the leading competitors had with him a coach/masseur, who asked him: "What event are you in, sonny?" Garfield told him and, not seeing him as a rival, the coach gave his arm and shoulder a rub down and offered some advice. Garfield's subsequent throw carried to where the field started to dip away, taking it even further. Also that year he was Glamorgan youth discus champion, then British Army Cadet discus and javelin champion in 1951. He went on to become 1951 Glamorgan javelin champion and 1953 Welsh champion, representing the Welsh Amateur Athletic Association between 1951 and 1954.

Schoolboy heroics in cricket and athletics surprisingly did not transfer in the same degree to his rugby. As lynchpin of the school team he was selected for the Welsh trials, but was unable to make enough impact to be picked for the team.

At Cowbridge, it was Mr Rees who was a central character in much of his success, rather than the new PE master, another who had returned from war service in 1945. It was the PE master who coached Garfield for the school athletic championships, but the teacher had seen some action in the war and suffered for it, turning up at school the worse for wear from drink at times. He asked to see Garfield's solid silver medal after one year's championships, and took it away for engraving, but Garfield never saw it again. He often pondered on whether it was lost, or sold to pay for drink, but never pushed the issue.

His cricket and rugby, meanwhile, were developing outside school. Garfield established himself in the first teams of both sports at Llanharan, often meaning two games in a day with his school commitments. That necessitated playing under an assumed name because the school did not approve of such practices. He also needed a pseudonym when playing for the Colliery cricket team. In 1950 the National Coal Board ran a knockout colliery competition for the area. The Llanharan Colliery side consisted mainly of the Llanharan cricket team, most of them being employed there, although Garfield, of course, was not. The cup was won, Ogilvie Colliery being beaten in the final, thus bringing to the village the first (and only) cup ever won by the local side. Noted rugby journalist J.B.G. Thomas later commented on Garfield's cricket in the *Western Mail*, saying he had cricketer's hands, with "the instinct for forming the perfect cradle for the ball. He is able to throw a cricket ball prodigious distances, and bowls cutters with a swift arm action." He tried cricket at a higher level by joining the Cowbridge club, where Glamorgan had played a few county matches in the early 1930s. Glamorgan had been county champions in 1948 so were quite an attraction to him, but he soon realised he would never be good enough for county cricket and gave it up to concentrate more on athletics.

Welsh rugby union in the 1950s, like elsewhere, was not divided into official leagues, with the authorities frowning on teams becoming too competitive. There were still different levels, of course, and at a higher level than Llanharan in the local area was Maesteg, tucked in just below the really top-flight clubs. The Old Parish, as they were known, were a long-established club in another mining area, and had a fine team. Included in their ranks was Trevor Lloyd, a Welsh international scrum-half, one of many great players they had produced, some of whom had turned to rugby league. They were at the peak of their form, with 1949–50 becoming known as the 'Invincible Season'. Being just a few miles from Llanharan, they had noted Garfield's promise and invited him on occasion to guest for them, in return for two shillings for the bus fare up the valley. It was not always just two shillings. After a late call-up to a match against Nuneaton he went to the treasurer's office to collect his expenses, but because of his late selection there was no envelope bearing his name. When Garfield explained the situation the treasurer tipped his cash box upside down and gave him its entire contents, which amounted to 18 shillings and 10 pence ha' penny – about £22 in 2011 terms.

Maesteg's successes continued with Garfield in the side. They won the first five games of the 1950–51 season to extend their unbeaten run to 52 matches, before losing to Bridgend on 23 September. Their centenary book recorded that "Trevor Lloyd and Viv Callow were still a splendid pair of half-backs, and the pack were, for the most part, still intact and going great guns. Among those who played during the season were Bryn Phillips, Viv Dixon, Tommy Llewellyn and Garfield Owen, a young Llanharan full-back."

His performances for Maesteg fuelled his ambition. What he really wanted to do now was play for a top side. It was nothing to do with money – all union clubs were strictly amateur. Expenses might be slightly better, and he had heard talk of boot money, but that was far from his mind. What he wanted was to be noticed. Cardiff and

Newport were the major clubs in the region, consistently good on the field and always well represented in the international squad. Llanharan had an understanding with Newport that they would point up-and-coming juniors in their direction – a sort of feeder club in the modern sense – but in 1951 Cardiff appeared to him to be the better option. It was nearer home, and he knew some of their younger players from school matches and trials, so went along with them to training. He was picked for the second team, known as Cardiff Athletic or The Rags, and played a few games for them, but that was soon not possible.

With schooldays having come to an end at the same time, thoughts turned to future plans. He had worked during the school holidays over the years delivering milk, which in those days came in churns for tipping out into jugs, as well as on a farm, and underground in the colliery with his father. He had also been down the pit when in the process of writing a thesis on different types of mining for his sixth-form studies at school. These were all jobs that he was now sure he did not want to do. His sporting skills seemed to allow him to get away with taking it easy, so his initial thinking had been that the best way of continuing his current lifestyle would be to stay in education. University places were scarce in 1951. Garfield had not put too much emphasis on the academic side of school life so his qualifications were not quite good enough, but they were good enough for teacher training college, a growth area in the years after the war. Some of his friends were heading to college in Birmingham, and he was inclined to join them. Another possibility, however, was the army, two years National Service being a legal requirement in the 1950s. His original plan had been to leave this until completing college. However, the Royal Artillery, based at Oswestry in Shropshire, just over the border with North Wales, were looking to build up the strength of their rugby union side. They had written to Cowbridge Grammar School asking that good players be pointed in their direction. When Garfield was told about this, the idea appealed. It seemed sensible to go where he would be wanted, and where he could still continue to spend much of his time playing sport, even though it would put at least a temporary end to his time with Cardiff.

During his early years and schooldays his working-class upbringing had allowed no airs and graces, though he had tried often enough. Now he was moving to a new phase of his life, which would eventually present opportunities to subconsciously climb the social ladder a little more.

Garfield's father as captain of Llanharan, 1926–27. His uncle Dilwyn is in the back row. Back: J. Goodman, D. Evans, D. Owen, T. Sheldon, W. Blanche; middle: D. Hughes, I. Scourfield, G. Brewer, B. Frowen, R. Evans, L. Frowen, M. Edmunds, W. Thomas (secretary); front: L. Thomas, G. Perkins, J. Owen, T. Davies, L. Cogbill.

Llanharan Army Cadet squad. Garfield second left, Brian Sparks fourth left.

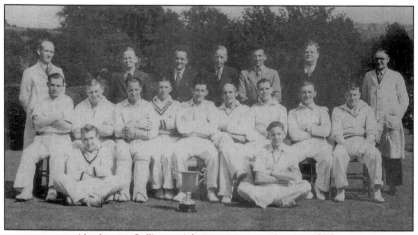

Llanharan Colliery cricket team, cup winners 1950.
Back: T. Farrel (umpire), officials V.S. Parry, R. Davies, G.D. Corfield,
J.S. Hughes, T. Jones, C. Hadley (umpire); middle: R.J. Piggott, M. Saunders,
C. Shellibeer, R. Towell, W. Roderick, M. Cogbill, W. Bowden, A. Preece,
G. Pascoe; front: G. Owen (playing as E.T. Lewis), D. Thomas.

Cowbridge Grammar School 1st XV, 1950–51.
Back: L.B. Hill, R. Morris, J. Evans, R. Cornwell, D.M. Williams, R. Roberts,
W.G. Price, K. Rees, H. Clayton; front: P.D. Robins, D.H. Rowlands,
B.H. Rowlands (vice-captain), G.D. Owen (captain), D.L. Jones,
R. Cattanach, A. Ghose.

# 2. The calm before the storm

The first fortnight with the 17th Training Regiment at Oswestry was spent doing drill. His sporting skills worked to his advantage again, as it had been suggested they would. The Welsh quartermaster sergeant who ran the gymnastics at the camp lined up the new recruits and asked if any of them played for a rugby club. Garfield replied "Cardiff", which aroused great interest and he was given a rugby ball to kick down the park. He could not have been asked to do anything more appropriate. "You're staying here," he was told, for most of the group was moving on to the 67th Regiment. Army pay was seven shillings and sixpence to start with, of which two shillings and sixpence was sent home as an overdue contribution to the family. The pay progressed to 15 shillings (75p – the equivalent of around £17 in 2011) by the end, when he had become a PTI (Physical Training Instructor), and given the rather unimaginative nickname of "Taff". As Lance Bombardier G.D. Owen, he won representative honours with the Western Command and Royal Artillery XVs during these two years, against opponents such as the Royal Engineers and the Duke of Wellington's Regiment. Playing colleagues included Sid Lowden, latterly of Workington Town RLFC, and Leeds rugby league stand-off Gordon Brown.

Army matches were infrequent, so Garfield looked elsewhere for games. The nearest rugby club to Oswestry was Wrexham, who were also on the lookout for players to improve their team. Weekends were free time, when the rest of the regiment lazed around or went home, but for Garfield the more rugby the better. He went off on the bus to play for Wrexham, and became an influential member of the team. Wrexham tended to keep the ball in the forwards, but did have a move called 'hot potato' which involved spinning the ball wide, with Garfield coming up to create the extra man outside the inappropriately named centre Cliff Forward. It helped make for some enjoyable rugby.

Playing for Wrexham qualified him to represent North Wales in the Welsh County Championship Cup. In his second season, 1952–53, he figured for them in the first round victory over Cardigan on his new home ground of Rhosnessney on Wednesday 11 February, and in the semi-final defeat at his former ground Maesteg against Glamorgan on Wednesday 15 April. Five team-mates from Wrexham, Cliff Forward, Cadfan Davies, J. Roberts, R.G. Williams and K. Avery were in the team with him. Three years later he was to guest for another North Wales County XV for a celebration match at Colwyn Bay against a Welsh Rugby Union XV to mark the 25th anniversary of the formation

Royal Artillery and Royal Engineers rugby union squads – Garfield is third right in the back row, Gordon Brown second right in the front row.

of the North Wales Rugby Union. Garfield kicked a goal, but according to press reports had to make several "flying tackles to stop the South Wales wingers" as their superior opponents easily beat them 30–8 in front of 1,500 spectators. There was a celebration dinner afterwards at the Metropole Hotel in the town.

A festival of rugby in Bournemouth led to problems in 1952, when he was invited to play there with Llanharan. Being spread over several days, he needed permission from the Army for leave, and coincidentally a day or two later found himself talking in the gym to the Colonel, a rugby enthusiast who said that of course he could go. That was apparently not the correct way to do things and his Sergeant Major, who he should have asked first, marched him to his office. "I've already replied that you're not going," he said. "Now I'll have to write again and say that you are!" A dressing down followed, and two hours in the glasshouse[*].

The tournament was a success for Llanharan, who enjoyed notable wins over teams like Oxford Woodpeckers and H.M.S. Raleigh, a Royal Navy training establishment in the south west. *Welsh Rugby* magazine, in an article on the Llanharan club in February 1975, recorded that in the festival matches Llanharan scored 10 tries, but Garfield did not convert any of them. "I even missed the ones under the posts," he remembers. Completion of National Service in 1953 necessitated new plans, with rugby again predominant in his mind. Home in South

---

[*] Army prison

Left: Last day at Oswestry, 1953.
Above: Javelin champion

Wales, where the family had moved house to nearby Llanharry, the obvious choice was to go back to Cardiff. When he thought about it carefully though, Cardiff seemed well catered for with full-backs; so it seemed more sensible to try Newport. The black-and-ambers were in a golden era with stellar performers in Roy Burnett, Ken Jones, Bryn Meredith and Malcolm Thomas, and crowds in their thousands were flocking to watch. Although there were no leagues to judge them by, the newspapers produced unofficial tables from all matches the clubs played, and Newport were generally around the top despite a tougher fixture list than most.

He went along to the trials at the start of the season, only to find them washed out by a thunderstorm. They were rearranged, but before he had a chance to get settled with Newport, there were decisions about his future career to be made, and teacher training college was back on the agenda.

A friend from Llanharan, Dorio Lusardi, another keen rugby player, was at Shoreditch College, and encouraged Garfield to join him there. It was another case of an institution wanting to build up a rugby team and he was welcomed onto the course. The college was no longer in

London's Shoreditch, which is on the fringes of the City of London and the East End. It had relocated in 1951 to a new home 27 miles away on a much larger site in a semi-rural spot at Cooper's Hill, Englefield Green, Surrey, on the outskirts of Egham. The 60 acres of beautiful grounds on a hill overlooking the Thames and Runnymede later became Brunel University's Runnymede Campus. He had a room there, shared in his first year, but on his own in the second, a pleasant change after the communal barracks at Oswestry. Shoreditch was famed at the time for woodwork, which Garfield did, but he was never going to be a woodwork teacher; the course was merely a means to an end, the end being to play sport. Thoughts of playing for Newport, now too far away, were put on hold and he turned out instead for the Shoreditch College XV, alongside such as Dorio and Howard Jones, a scrum-half from Llanelli who could play a bit. Also in the team at centre was Dai Williams, a quality tennis player with whom he became good friends, and was later to be best man at his wedding.

In the summer Garfield figured prominently in the cricket team, but achieved even more success with athletics. In his first year at the Inter-College Athletics Championships, he secured first place in putting the shot, second place in throwing the javelin and third place in the discus throw. In his second year he won both the shot putt event and the javelin, setting up a new record with a throw of 175 feet 11 inches, almost enough for full international selection. As at school, his studies took on a secondary role to the sport, but he did what he had to do on the two-year course, his experience as a PTI in the Army helping greatly with the teaching practice element.

The social scene was limited, there being no bar at the college, but the local Barley Mow pub filled the space, becoming the scene of much bonhomie. There were also dances, at one of which in May 1954 he met Marlene Sternson, who would become his wife. Marlene was on a state scholarship studying mathematics at Royal Holloway College, sited just a few hundred yards away. Despite Garfield being forever away at the weekends playing sport, the relationship flourished. Marlene, a Londoner who had been evacuated to Wales in the war years, was fond of watching sport and went with him to the Oxford versus Cambridge varsity match at Twickenham, which was only 16 miles away. Twickenham was the Mecca for English Rugby Union supporters, though neither of them were over-impressed with either the stadium as a whole or the long grass on a playing surface surrounded by piles of straw.

Garfield had been there earlier for the Wales versus England international on 16 January 1954, this time with student friends in the back of a Morris Minor van. It was the first match of the season's international championship, Wales being strongly fancied after a recent win over the New Zealand All Blacks, and having won the Triple Crown and Grand Slam in 1951–52, followed by three of their four fixtures in 1952–53. For Welshmen, the England match was the one that mattered most, and they had not lost at Twickenham since 1939. It was the first ever all-ticket international to be staged there and tickets were hard to come by, but Garfield had secured some from Llanharan RFC at not inconsiderable cost. The students were in high spirits; before the match he and another raced onto the field passing a leek between them, then ran over to where the band was providing the pre-match entertainment and proceeded to conduct them. Had it been a football match today they would probably have been arrested, but nobody showed any concern and they returned happily to the terraces to watch the match. Left winger Gwyn Rowlands scored a try and penalty goal for Wales, but full-back Gerwyn Williams damaged his shoulder tackling England's Ted Woodward, and Billy Williams and Rex Willis both also needed treatment for injuries. The teams were locked at 6–6 when a last-minute try by England winger Chris Winn sent the students back to college dejected.

There were repercussions on the following Monday morning, when the college principal called them to his office. He had seen their antics on the field. "I want no more of that," he said. "The next time I see you on that pitch, Owen, is when you're playing."

Such a possibility became a whole lot closer just a few months later. When home from college for the holidays, he turned out for Llanharan and, when needed, Maesteg. Easter Monday 1954 saw him playing for Maesteg, at the end of a period when he played five or six games in a fortnight including his additional commitments to college. On arriving home, he was told that Newport official Vincent Griffiths had phoned, asking him to play for them the following day against the Barbarians, the famous invitation side who were completing their Easter tour. Newport had played that day at home to London Welsh and, as well as losing the match 15–11, also lost full-back Gary Legge, centre John Roblin and fly-half Roy Burnett to injury. Vincent Griffiths was an influential figure in Welsh rugby union, and had seen Garfield play in the Newport trial at the beginning of the season, as well as a few years earlier when he had visited Llanharan, canvassing votes for his place on the Welsh RU committee. He had also heard glowing reports from others who had spotted Garfield's talent. Now that Griffiths needed a full-back, he remembered him.

This was a big moment, the chance of a first appearance in top-class rugby union, but when Garfield rang him back, ever the honest gentleman, he pointed out his recent heavy playing commitments and suggested that as he might not be able to give his best they might like to contact someone else. The reply was that if they could have

17

thought of anyone else to ring they would already have done that. After such a response he could hardly refuse and his Newport debut was fixed. Up to now, National Service and teacher training college had combined to stifle his ambition, but all of a sudden the opportunity had arrived. It was time for him to deliver. Could he produce the goods when it really mattered?

A Llanharan contingent followed him to the ground at Rodney Parade to watch the match, including his father, former schoolteacher Gwyn Williams, and several of his club-mates. They were amused before the game at the somewhat vitriolic remarks of a section of the Newport supporters standing near them, who were slating their club selectors for playing an unknown in such an important game, and rallied to his defence.

The rest of the team were well-seasoned performers, including seven current or future Welsh internationals. The full Newport side was: Garfield Owen, Ken Jones, Brian Jones, John Lane, Graham Ross, Malcolm Thomas, Onllwyn Brace, Bryn Meredith, Lyn Davies, Harold Davies, Ian Ford, Malcolm Quartley, Doug Ackerman, Dick Sheppard, Leighton Jenkins.

The Barbarians fielded 13 internationals in their star-studded line up: Viv Evans (Wales), B.M. Gray, Phil Davies (England), Paul Johnstone (South Africa), Thomas Weatherstone (Scotland), Jack Kyle (Ireland), John Williams (England), Hugh McLeod (Scotland), Eric Evans (England), Courtenay Meredith (Wales), Tom Reid (Ireland), H.B. Nealy, Chuck Henderson (Scotland), Robin Thompson (Ireland), Dyson Wilson (England).

Newspaper reports show that the match was only seconds old when Garfield gathered a high punt with his usual nonchalant grace and slammed the ball into touch three-parts of the way down the touchline. From that moment the crowd took him to their hearts. One notable tackle on Barbarian Phil Davies (or W.P.C. Davies as he was more commonly known in the rugby union tradition of referring to players with more common surnames by their initials) left the heavy, craggy England international centre in a heap as Newport triumphed 14–3. Garfield's goalkicking had not been utilised; Brian Jones landed the one conversion, and Onllwyn Brace a drop-goal. The tries came from John Lane, Doug Ackerman (the father of Rob, a British Lion who turned to rugby league with Whitehaven and played for several clubs) and Dick Sheppard. At the end of the game Garfield happily signed scores of autograph books thrust at him by eager young admirers. Significantly, among those to congratulate him was Vincent Griffiths.

The national press joined the praise. With the headline "Student hits Baa-Baas", the *Daily Express* said that "Garfield Owen made his debut at full-back for Newport and came near to being the star of the match. In the stiffest test he could have had, he made good." Garfield himself didn't think much of it at the time, preferring in his modest way to talk down the standard of the opposition. "They do a lot of drinking on these tours, you know!" he says, but his performance made an impression at Newport. They now rated him as a player, and chose him for the following Saturday's match at Abertillery. One more appearance came before the end-of-season match at Llanelli when, according to the *South Wales Argus,* he "came off the field with some glory added to his increasing reputation. He fielded and tackled well, and looks as if he has a long future with the club."

The lack of an official league system allowed clubs like Newport to build up a fixture list that could incorporate matches not just against Welsh teams, but against English opposition, and allow for tours away in a crowded but varied programme. Although every match was played to win, it was also for fun, friendship and frivolity, especially in England, where fixtures with Harlequins, Gloucester, Wasps and the like provided opportunities to throw the ball around. Indeed this was very much how Garfield looked at the game. "It was not about winning and losing for me," he says. "It was about playing the game." Yet the contests against sides from the valleys were ultra-competitive, fiercely combative affairs, made so by intense local pride. The Newport versus Cardiff clashes could stand comparison with any Wigan versus St Helens rugby league encounter.

There were generally four such matches each season, as they generated much income from huge attendances. "Few outsiders ever realise the competitive nature of Welsh club rugby," wrote David Watkins, a later Newport player, in his autobiography. "A Newport match against Neath or Bridgend or Llanelli or, of course, against Cardiff, is a mini-international. Even regular spectators cannot know the tension and the will to win engendered in the dressing room." Matches against supposedly weaker clubs could be just as demanding; for such as Abertillery, Newbridge or Ebbw Vale to beat Newport would be a highlight of their season.

In previews for the 1954–55 season in the Welsh press, Garfield suddenly shot to prominence. *Football Echo* correspondent Dave Phillips named him as one of the best three prospects in Welsh rugby. At 5 feet 8 inches tall and weighing 13 stones, he had a good build, some describing him as stocky and others as chunky. His defence was a huge strength, because he had become proficient in offering the opposing player the touchline then bringing him down from the side, concentrating on the relaxed, trailing leg. Coupled with top-class touch-finding – these were the days when the ball could be kicked directly off the park from anywhere – and as yet unseen goalkicking, he had in abundance the major skills to make a success of the full-back role.

Newport had experienced more problems with full-back than any other position the previous year. Malcolm Lewis had started the season there, and Peter Smith had a spell before Gary Legge took over. The time was right for Garfield. For the pre-season trial match he was only selected for the 'Possibles', against the cream of the Newport squad, but things turned out well. *South Wales Argus* correspondent Jack Davies wrote: "An outstanding feature of the trial was the unruffled efficiency of Garfield Owen, the full-back who played for Newport at the end of last season." In the showers afterwards he overheard his hero Ken Jones commenting favourably on his positional play. "I kicked the ball and he was under it, I tried to run it and he was there to tackle me." It all helped to build his confidence, and won him a place in the team.

He made a sparkling start to the season, impressing not only the Newport selectors but crucially also the press. The *South Wales Argus*, which covered all the matches, regularly singled him out for praise. In the unofficial season-opener against Rhymney Valley, it reported that Garfield "obviously thoroughly enjoyed himself to such an extent that long before the end he took on the extra role of third centre – and a very good one at that."

Newport Athletic Club First XV, 1954–55.
Back: R. Lewis (hon. trainer), B. Meredith, G. Keeley, J. Hancock, I. Ford,
J. Herrera, G. Morris, G. Whitson, G. Price, R.T. Carter (match hon. secretary);
middle: J. Lane, K. Jones, W.H. Bryant (chairman), M.C. Thomas (captain),
W.A. Everson (hon. secretary), D.A.G. Ackerman (vice-captain), G.D. Owen;
front: J. Roblin, B. Jones, H. Morgan, R. Burnett, D.O. Brace.

In the first official match he "played with supreme confidence in the face of all Bristol's attacks. Without him it is doubtful if Newport would have won." The next match they didn't, suffering a rare defeat at Neath, but "fair-haired Garfield Owen proved himself to be as steady in defence as his veteran opponent Viv Evans." His display was "the best individual performance of this fierce match. He fielded well, took grubber kicks in style, and if his kick lacked tremendous length, it had a comforting look of safety." His "shrewd knowledge of full-back technique saved Newport when all seemed lost. Once when Huins was approaching at top speed he brilliantly hedged him towards the touchline before executing a superb tackle, and then, in the last minutes, he brought off a mark which gave his side both a much needed breather and a large chunk of Neath ground." Garfield, the report concluded, "without doubt is the best Newport full-back for several seasons."

Another journalist, Dennis Busher, joined the praise. "22-year-old Garfield Owen looked the answer to Newport's full-back problems," he wrote. He also had noted his defence at Neath: "Two tackles, with Neath's fast wingmen John Huins and Keith Maddocks on the receiving end, proved that the supporter who told Newport about Owen after he had seen him play in a scratch Army side, was a good judge. Welsh javelin champion Owen has the shoulders and build that go with success in the sport. They seem to have the full-back find of the season."

And so it continued. Against Swansea "Owen at full-back was rarely in difficulties", then in his first match against arch-rivals Cardiff, "Owen, young and inexperienced as he is, was superbly calm under the strong pressure, putting in as polished a display by a Newport full-back as we have seen since before the war." Cardiff, entering the fray with a 100 per cent record from their first nine matches of the season, were held to a draw. Two players, the report concluded, influenced the 3–3 result, Garfield and Cardiff's Cliff Morgan. "The side without one of these might have lost."

Against Blackheath "Garfield Owen again played an immaculate game at full-back for Newport who were never in danger of defeat", spending an "exceptionally busy afternoon showing just how good a full-back he is." In the defeat of Gloucester he "rationed himself to one mistake, but by his imperturbable coolness at full-back bolstered up the whole side's confidence." Significantly in this match he took over the goalkicking role, previously the realm of Jack Hancock, an England international forward and later Salford rugby league player. "Since Garfield Owen kicked a penalty, converted two of the three tries and missed the other kick by inches, Newport also seem to have found an adequate deputy goalkicker to Jack Hancock, who was on army duty."

He was kicker again the following week, though not as successfully. "Garfield Owen missed a couple of goals before putting over an easy penalty goal, and later converted two of the tries. His goalkicking was not so good as it might have been, but, that apart, his play was stamped with reassuring competence and calmness."

Newport's season was progressing well, tucked in nicely just below Cardiff in the unofficial table. Garfield kicked another conversion in the next fixture at Llanelli at the end of October but, if a 16–8 defeat was a setback for the team, his own reputation continued to grow. The match report suggested that "perhaps the most interesting feature of a very good game was the strong duel between the full-backs. In striking contrast were the calm, competent, courageous but always orthodox methods of Newport's Garfield Owen, with the adventurous attacking tactics of Alun Thomas. Both were great, and there seems little doubt that the next Welsh full-back will be one of these two."

This was a new development. After just a couple of months of his first full season in top-class rugby union, he was being talked about in terms of international selection. It had been a meteoric rise.

In the 1950s, and indeed right through until as late as 1990, the Wales team was selected by the Welsh Rugby Union committee who, since the 1920s, had delegated the process to a special sub-committee known as 'The Big Five'. To most spectators and players these five men were remote people and in many respects considered gods, so it must have been of great help to Garfield that their chairman at the time was Newport's Vincent Griffiths, the man who had brought him to the club the previous Easter. He would have read all the reports, and presumably seen most of the performances for himself.

Garfield found himself being picked for the first Welsh trial at Ebbw Vale Welfare Ground in November. It was a great surprise for him. He was away during the week at college in England, unable even to train with Newport or mix with the supporters or hear the gossip. "People must have been talking about me, but I didn't realise," he recalls. This was another great opportunity though, a chance to progress to the very top of the sport.

# 3. Into the big time

It might seem strange to an outsider that an international team would be selected from trial matches, but they were a rugby union tradition that was not about to die out. It was a system that was to work in Garfield's favour, who was selected for the Reds, a side that included many of those who had figured in the Welsh team the previous season, when they had been the Five Nations Championship winners. Although they had lost when Garfield watched them against England 10 months ago, they had won 15, drawn one and lost just four of their championship matches during the 1950s. While they were not yet a great side, there were definite signs that they were moving in that direction.

Echoing the situation Garfield had encountered at Newport, one problematic area for Wales had been full-back, where the 'Big Five' had been unable to come up with a player who could hold down the position on a regular automatic basis. Garfield's performances for Newport suggested that he could be the player that Vincent Griffiths and his colleagues had been looking for. The trial was apparently a drab, lacklustre game in heavy, windswept conditions, but Garfield, given the goalkicking responsibilities, made the most of it as the Reds won 18–8. Headlines of the match reports included "Garfield Owen Discovery of First Trial", "Garry Owen's Kicks Highlight the Trial" and "Owen's Fine Kicking in Welsh Trial". Eynon Hammett recorded that "Garfield Owen, the young Newport full-back, staked a strong claim to international recognition by landing a forty-yard penalty goal and converting all three tries". Roland Stone was even more complimentary: "Owen, playing in only his 15th first-class game, can be marked a certainty for the second trial at Llanelli on December 11. In the first half he consistently made 50 yards or more with his touch kicks. In addition he kicked four goals from five kicks on a day when [opponents] the Whites landed only one of six attempts". Another reporter, in the *South Wales Echo*, added that he "played with all the aplomb of a veteran".

The second trial match was successfully negotiated, leaving the Final Trial, Probables versus Possibles, at Cardiff Arms Park on New Year's Day 1955. Garfield was in the Probables side. The Possibles' full-back was not Alun Thomas, as predicted by the *South Wales Argus*, but Arthur Edwards of London Welsh. Garfield's form held, so hopes were high of winning his first cap, but all he could do was wait until the Welsh Rugby Union announced the team a few days later.

Newport's three Welsh internationals in 1955: Garfield, Ken Jones and Bryn Meredith

Finally the news came through on the radio. Garfield's dream had come true. He had been selected to make his international debut for Wales, against England, at Cardiff Arms Park on 15 January.

Also in the team was 23-year-old Brian Sparks, who had been in the year above Garfield at Cowbridge Grammar School and a fellow Army Cadet, despite having only been in the Possibles side at the final trial. Sparks had been born in Llanharan like Garfield, but had moved away when he was young. It was a proud moment for headmaster Idwal Rees to see two of his old boys selected for the same Welsh side. He wrote to Garfield offering his congratulations. "Good luck for the day," he wrote, "We shall all be there." In typical headmaster style he added a tip: "I saw the trial on Saturday and I was horrified by the disastrous plight in which you were placed, first by a wild pass from Cliff Morgan, and then by a wild charge from the brainless R.C.C. Thomas who hit you right off balance as you were fielding. Should you find yourself in similar positions on the big day, make them know by a clear shout of 'Let it come' or 'Mine' that you are competent to deal with the job."

This was the age of the telegram – the Llanharan club sent one to Shoreditch to congratulate him, the first of scores of them, accompanied by phone calls of good wishes, from friends, associates and enthusiastic local supporters.

In addition to Brian Sparks, Garfield knew two others in the Wales selection well, his Newport club colleagues Ken Jones on the wing and Bryn Meredith at hooker. The rest he was briefly acquainted with, having met them at the trials. From his Probables team at the final trial, only centre Colin Bosley, second-row Rhys Williams and flanker Richard Thomas were missing, so he was reasonably familiar with his colleagues' play. That was fortunate, for there was no team get-together until a brief Friday evening session the day before the match, led by the team captain, in this case his hero Bleddyn Williams. Typically of the times, there was nothing in the way of a coach. There would be no overnight stay; it would be home on Friday night, then back to Cardiff again on the Saturday morning.

Former Welsh centre Wilfred Wooller once wrote in a *Boys Book of All Sports* that "nothing quite equals the thrill of playing for your country the first time. It has its anxious moments, especially in the days leading up to the match when a fear of breaking a leg or catching a serious illness dominates one's thoughts." For Garfield, those anxious days were to double. Annoyingly it began to snow, so heavy on the Friday that the already brief preparations were seriously disrupted. Training had to be abandoned after a token 20-minute snow-soccer match at Ely. Then, even more frustratingly, the snow failed to relent and the match itself had to be called off. How often did that happen! It was hastily rescheduled for seven days later, 22 January.

The weather eventually improved, though the thaw, followed by steady drizzle, made conditions wet and muddy for Friday's preparations, this time held at Glamorgan Wanderers' ground. If the previous week's events had been a let down for Garfield, they were nothing compared to this day. It was destined to end in heartbreak.

In attempting to retrieve a ball from the side of the field, he fell over the stump of a tree and damaged his left knee. It didn't seem too serious at the time, but on returning home there was clearly a problem and the family doctor was called. The bursa of his patella had been pierced and the fluid was leaking out. The doctor inserted a couple of stitches, but when asked about the match, said he did not think Garfield should try to play. Years later Brian Sparks echoed the thoughts of many when he said if it had been him he would have crawled on to the pitch to win his first cap, but Garfield knew what he would have to do. It might not have been a broken leg, but the fears of Wilfred Wooller were being played out. On Saturday morning the knee was stiff and swollen anyway, and the only decision he could make was to cry off.

At Llanharan railway station he gave the news to the crowds of supporters on the platform, then set off for the team's headquarters to make it official. He explained the injury and was told that the final decision whether to play rested with him. "I'm sorry, I can't play," he uttered resignedly to the selectors. These were the days before substitutes were permitted, and risks could not be taken. It was a decision that had to be made for the good of the team. His father was a bit upset about it all, and there was much disappointment around Llanharan and further afield. A supporter named Jack wrote to say, "Do you know, you made me miss my first Wales versus England match for years. When I knew you weren't playing, I just could not go to that ground and watch it. I was so bitterly disappointed I flogged my ticket and took a train to London and spent the weekend there. I

25

was in time to see the game on television in a pub in Woolwich. I got about as much a kick out of it as watching a funeral."

For Garfield himself it did not seem quite so bad, though he does admit to welling up and having to leave the changing rooms before kick-off when he saw his replacement, Arthur Edwards, pulling on what should have been his shirt. He was confident he would be selected again.

It was Arthur Edwards who kicked the penalty goal that won the match for Wales 3–0. Typically Garfield was the first man on the field at the end of the game, tip-toeing through the mud to shake his hand. The team masseur was shocked. "What did you do that for?" he asked, as Garfield scraped the mud from his shoes in the changing rooms. "Because he's had a good game," he replied. Back in Llanharan later that evening, he called in at the Welfare Hall to be given a spontaneous round of applause, and dragged to the microphone to say a few words. Edwards retained his place for the Scotland match at Murrayfield a fortnight later, when scrum-half Rex Willis took over from Bleddyn Williams as captain, but this time Wales lost 14–8, beaten by a Scotland side that had suffered 15 consecutive championship defeats over four seasons. In some ways it was a match best missed, though Garfield never again had the opportunity to play at Murrayfield. He felt he was just about fit and could have played, but he had dropped out of Newport's team the previous Saturday and did not play for them on the day of the Scotland match either or even the next week. His place was taken by reserve full-back John Hughes.

There would be team changes for the next match against Ireland, which was not due until five weeks later, giving Garfield the opportunity to prove his fitness in club matches against Cardiff on 19 February and 5 March. In the first he took a worrying knock: "Very badly shaken early in the game, Garfield Owen carried on obviously in pain, but gave Cardiff no chance to exploit any weaknesses", said one report, though his team were beaten 6–0. The second match was at Cardiff Arms Park, where a huge crowd witnessed Newport's revenge, their first victory there since 1951, by 11–6. His knee had survived both stern tests.

The evening of the team announcement arrived with Garfield 135 miles away at college. His mates kept him up until the early hours of the morning, when one of them, John Lewis, used the college payphone to contact the *Daily Express* for details of the team. At first the newspaper was reluctant to divulge the information, but eventually told him that Owen was the Wales Number 1 – in those days the Welsh, like England and Scotland, numbered their shirts in the same manner as rugby league. Non-drinker Garfield retired to bed happy, leaving his mates to continue their celebrations. The next day he found that lock-forward Rees Stephens had been made captain and the threequarter line had been altered, but the important thing was that he would at last be able to win his cap on 12 March at Cardiff Arms Park.

In the following days there were a couple of important letters in his pigeon hole. The first was from Vincent Griffiths: "This note is just to confirm the news in the paper – you are now officially included in the XV – unless you try some foolish prank like falling over a tree stump." The second, from the Welsh RU, was a nicely printed selection card, together with a duplicated sheet which brought news of practice on the Friday at 4.00pm, and a request to report for lunch at the Royal Hotel, Cardiff, on the Saturday at 12.15pm. "You are to play in black polished boots and white shorts," it said. "You are entitled to one complimentary grandstand ticket and one at purchase price (15/-)". It added that with selection against France also likely, "you had better see, as soon as possible, that your passport is in order". There was a note at the bottom, "Your selection is a condition that you show yourself to be fit on Saturday".

This time there were no last-minute mishaps, and Garfield was able to pull on the Welsh shirt for the first time. There was no game plan, which suited him down to the ground; he had always played for enjoyment, sharing the contemporary belief that coaching inhibited flair. He had rarely had the opportunity to join training sessions at Maesteg, Wrexham or Newport, so this was what he was familiar with.

The Arms Park in 1955 had strictly limited facilities for players as well as spectators, and the field was a mud-heap with grass four or five-inch long, nothing like the immaculate conditions at Cardiff's Millennium Stadium today. He was used to that, having played there for Newport and in the trial, but this time was special as the crowds thronged from the neighbouring city-centre streets and pubs to loudly support their beloved Wales.

Inside, despite there being a greyhound track around the outside of the playing area, the atmosphere was spine-tingling and unique. Once the roar started when Wales attacked, it was impossible to hear the referee's whistle, and the crowd surges with only flimsy-looking barriers to hold them back, seemed dangerous and frightening. The villagers of Llanharan who could not get to the game crowded round their wireless sets, as a capacity crowd and brilliant sunshine saw Garfield give Wales the lead on 19 minutes. "Garfield Owen took great care with his penalty kick on the 25-yard line and about 10 yards in, and gave Wales the lead with a magnificent kick, the ball seeming to veer inside the near upright after threatening to go wide," reported the *South Wales Echo*.

Garfield had never been troubled with nerves, but it must have been a tricky moment. Ireland equalised after half-time, but a four-try blitz in the final quarter of an hour from Courtenay Meredith, Gareth Griffiths, Haydn Morris and Cliff Morgan, three of them converted by Garfield, saw Wales home by a flattering 21–3.

Apart from his goalkicking, he had not been happy with his own performance, feeling he had missed touch too often with his clearing kicks. J.B.G. Thomas in the *Western Mail* reported that "At full-back P. Berkery was better than G. Owen, although the new Welsh cap kicked nine of the 21 points. The Irishman showed a better sense of position, and I felt Owen was over-anxious. But conditions were not easy for full-back play, with a strong wind, bright sun and a light ball."

Afterwards, as after all international matches, there was a formal dinner. These were not held at the grounds, which did not have the facilities for such sumptuous events, but at a hotel. For Wales in 1955 this meant the Royal Hotel in St Mary Street, Cardiff, just a few minutes walk away. The five-course meal would be followed by speeches from the officials and captains of both teams, with a few drinks afterwards. One of the selectors came across to speak to Garfield there, it quickly becoming apparent that he had mistaken him for Bleddyn Williams. "I think we should keep the same team for the next match," he said once they had finished their discussion, "except for Owen."

Fortunately this view was not shared by his colleagues, who voted to retain him for the last match of the campaign against France at Stade Colombes in Paris on 26 March. This was something of an adventure, Garfield meeting up with the rest of the party for luncheon at the Grosvenor Hotel in London at 12 noon on the Thursday. The others had travelled from Cardiff by train to Paddington, where a private coach had transferred them to the hotel at Victoria. The afternoon train took them to Folkestone harbour and a steamer to Calais, with tea on the boat, then a train to Paris and dinner in the restaurant car. Finally a coach carried them to the hotel at St Lazare. On the Friday there was a practice session at Colombes in the afternoon, then at night a visit to the Casino de Paris – not as the name might suggest a gambling house, but one of Paris's well-known music halls.

Departure for the match was at 1.30pm on Saturday for the 3.30pm kick-off, with Wales needing victory for a share of the title. Points difference was not introduced as a consideration until as late as 1994 but, if it had counted, a victory by more than four points would have been enough to top the championship table. Such tables had less significance in rugby union circles in 1955, and to Garfield too they were of minor importance, but to many players and fans they meant everything.

France were formidable opponents. They had already beaten Scotland, Ireland and England, so were in search of the Grand Slam. The crunch match even had its sentimental side as well, for French captain Jean Prat, an inspiration since shortly after the war, had announced his retirement and this was his last championship fixture. A record crowd of 62,000 assembled.

The Stade Colombes was France's largest stadium. It had been used for the 1924 Olympic Games, where Eric Liddell and Harold Abrahams had won the 100 metres and 400 metres races depicted in the film *Chariots of Fire*. It had expanded since then to a capacity of 60,000 and was the home of the French national team until the renovated Parc des Princes was inaugurated in 1972. It also hosted many of France's international association football matches. The place was noisy and exuberant, and intimidating to visiting players.

This was to be a great Welsh performance though, their powerful forwards denying the dangerous French backs the ball. Garfield was able to convert both tries – from Alun Thomas and Haydn Morris – and, to an accompaniment of cat-calls and continuous whistling, add two 45-yard penalty goals as his team won 16–11. The Frenchman in charge of the scoreboard, maybe unable to believe the evidence of his own eyes, insisted on hoisting the figure of 14 instead of 16 against the name of Wales, leaving it at that to the bitter end. Garfield remembers one of his penalties vividly, as the ball seemed to be missing by about 15 yards until some Welsh divine spirit inexplicably altered its flight and sent it between the posts. A national newspaper strike meant restricted coverage, it being left to the Welsh press to record later that he had "played a blinder against France". French reports described him as a "maitre buteur", a master kicker. Wales had their share of the championship, the five-point victory enough to have given them the title outright under modern regulations. Jean Prat was chaired from the field, not by the dejected Frenchmen who may have been thinking there was still a friendly match against Italy for him to play, but by the Welsh – Alun Thomas and Gareth Griffiths to the fore.

The after-match banquets on Saturday evening in Paris were renowned occasions, with visiting teams generally having the times of their lives. This one at Restaurant Ledoyen on the Champs Élysées was to be no exception, though many of the French players failed to turn up. They had been expected to win the match, but their party had been spoilt in more ways than one.

Garfield's club rugby with Newport continued to go well. He featured in 24 matches, of which 18 were won and two drawn. The team as a whole was really strong, well-stocked with internationals

The Barbarians on their 1955 Easter Tour,
with Garfield front row fourth from right.

Wales versus Ireland at Cardiff, 1955. Back: A.I. Dickie (referee), L. Davies,
B. Meredith, R.H. Williams, R. Robins, R.C.C. Thomas, C. Meredith, I. Jones
(touch judge); middle: A. Thomas, K.J. Jones, J.R.G. Stephens, W.O. Williams,
H. Morris; front: G. Owen, G. Griffiths, C. Morgan, W.R. Willis.

Idwal Rees at a presentation by Llanharan RFC to Garfield on winning his Welsh cap. Among those present are the chairman of the selectors, Vincent Griffiths, Garfield's dad (3rd left) and his mum (3rd right).

The Committee have pleasure in informing

G. Owen.

that he has been selected to play for Wales against England, at Cardiff, on 15th January, 1955. Information about the arrangements for the match will be sent in due course.

*Secretary*

The debut that never was - the official selection card issued by the Welsh Rugby Union.

and Monmouthshire county representatives. Garfield himself, living away from the area, won no further county honours, despite some talk of him representing Surrey. Two of the newcomers – centre Harry Morgan, a Cambridge blue, and back-rower Geoff Whitson – were soon to also join the Wales ranks, while towards the end of the campaign the team was further bolstered by Vic Leadbetter, an England international the previous season when with Edinburgh Wanderers. Most of the players stuck around for years, for the team spirit at Newport in the 1950s was one of the club's strengths.

Garfield quickly became a 'stay-at-home' type of full-back, though it had not always been so. In earlier days he had occasionally enjoyed running out of defence if the opportunity arose, and linking with the attack as an extra man. Such play was pushed to the back of his mind following an incident in an early match when he had caught a failed penalty attempt near the posts. "Touch it down," called the captain, but the opponents were nowhere near and it seemed better to make ground by running with it. So he ignored the call, set off upfield, then kicked deep into touch when challenged. It seemed like good play, but the captain was furious – the message he was giving was that Garfield was running away from his support, a dangerous thing to do. He thereafter more-or-less permanently adopted the more conservative approach which became his trademark. With no coach as such, it was the captain who ran things. "It was down to us basically, nobody was trying to mould us," he recalls.

After his successes with the boot in the trials and his matches with Wales, he began to be used more often in that role by Newport, landing 17 conversions and 10 penalty goals for a total of 64 points by the end of the season. The club tried to help by having a local cobbler make for him a special pair of boots with a square toe, which he continued to use for a few years despite them making little noticeable difference to his success rate.

Being still a student in far-off Surrey, there was much travelling to be done even for home games. He would need to be up at 5.30am; the long train journey required two changes, then a quick walk to get him to the ground 90 minutes before kick-off. Fortunately the service was reliable. After the matches it would be smartly off to the station and back to college, arriving at 3am on Sunday. The Newport club looked after him well though, particularly the match secretary Nick Carter, who took him under his wing and was happy to pay for overnight hotel accommodation and taxi fares to and from the station, when all Garfield actually paid for was his return train ticket, his bicycle taking care of the rest of the journey. A friend of the club also paid for his college books, because Garfield did not qualify for a government grant, his parents footing the rest of his bills.

Towards the end of April, Newport toured Devon to complete their season, playing Plymouth Albion on the Saturday, Devonport Services on the Monday, and Exeter on Tuesday 26 April. The Easter holidays from Shoreditch were still in full swing, so Garfield was able to join them. The party left Newport at 5.45pm on the Friday, travelled by coach to Bristol, train to Plymouth, then coach to the Duke of Cornwall Hotel. The three matches were all won, 11–3 against both Plymouth Albion and Devonport Services, and 14–4 against Exeter Chiefs. Garfield played in all three, kicking three conversions and two penalties. On Tuesday they moved to the Cullompton Hotel, from where they travelled home on the Wednesday.

Touring was becoming commonplace, after he was also selected for the Barbarians squad for their Easter tour, based at the Esplanade Hotel in Penarth, playing in the matches against Swansea and Penarth, but opposing The Barbarians for Newport on the Tuesday. That must have seemed a strange experience, especially the ending, which might have won him some brownie points with the tourists. One report said that "It was poetic justice that Garfield Owen should miss the goalkick that might have given a two point victory over the Barbarians, for such a result would have presented an altogether distorted version of a great game" though "sure-footed, sure-handed, and calm in everything he did except for that last kick, Owen played superbly."

With selection for the Barbarians based on high standard of play and good behaviour on and off the field, it was a great honour, which was repeated the following season, when he appeared against Swansea and Cardiff. Barbarians matches were great social occasions, with dinners and golf tournaments arranged around them. Garfield joined the golfers at Penarth Golf Club at 10.30am on the Sunday after his first match for a four-ball competition, the players being split into groups of experienced players and novices. Being his first time on a course, Garfield was among the latter and watched as his partner's tee-shot finished close to the green, leaving him to take it from there. His chip amazingly trickled into the hole, bringing forth friendly howls of protest at his claimed beginner status.

Thereafter, whenever he bumped into Barbarian official Micky Steele-Bodger he was greeted with, "It's the guy who said he couldn't play golf!" In the clubhouse afterwards, he learned that there was a Rugby International Golf Society, which sounded like something he could get involved with, but during his playing days the Welsh never seemed to get organised for things like that. "You never really knew where you were with them. It was all far away when I was at College," he remembers. But golf was a sport that he was to return to later.

A British Lions tour, to South Africa, beckoned at the end of the season. The selectors, as always, sent letters to all prospective tourists to check on their availability. For most international rugby union players, in good jobs with supportive or sympathetic employers, this would be no problem, but for Garfield it was. He was still at Shoreditch College and would need the permission of the authorities there to travel. The principal, speaking like the typical old-fashioned schoolteacher who advised his pupils not to concentrate on sport, said, "If you take my advice, Garfield, your career comes first." So with permission not forthcoming, he had to reply saying he was unavailable. He would never know if he would have been selected, but it seems unlikely that he would have been omitted from a squad of 30.

Dave Phillips of the *South Wales Echo and Express* certainly thought he would have been in: "Asked for my own ideas of a Welsh contingent, I would plump for Rex Willis as skipper, with Cliff Morgan, Garfield Owen, Gareth Griffiths and Alun Thomas as backs, and the two Merediths, W.O. Williams, Russell Robins and Clem Thomas as strong forward candidates." Maybe Garfield might have eschewed his normal honesty and waited for selection before crying off.

Eleven Welsh players either had none of Garfield's problems, or managed to overcome them somehow. The miners and lorry drivers, he discovered, left their requests late, when it would have seemed heartless of their employers to refuse. Bryn Meredith, Courtenay Meredith, Russell Robins, Clem Thomas, Rhys Williams and Billy Williams were among the forwards, with Cliff Morgan, Gareth Griffiths, Trevor Lloyd, Haydn Morris and Alun Thomas in the backs. The tourists faced a winger, Tom van Vollenhoven, who scored a hat-trick of tries in the second test in Cape Town and would join St Helens RLFC in 1957, but recovered to draw the series 2–2, the first time since 1896 that a British side had avoided defeat in South Africa.

They might have fared even better with Garfield's full-back and goalkicking skills. The full-backs in the test matches were England's Douglas Baker, normally a fly-half, and Scotland's Angus Cameron, who had played full-back for Scotland a couple of times but was also more often at fly-half or centre. Garfield had to be content like the rest of the rugby fans back home with a minor share in the drama, as newsreel pictures at cinemas and on television showed the epic series unravel. Three of the tourists later signed for rugby league clubs, Irish skipper Robin Thompson and English back Martin Regan joined Warrington and England centre Pat Quinn signed for Leeds.

Garfield remained in the selectors' thoughts. The following New Year's Eve he played with many of the tourists in a combined England-Wales XV which beat Scotland-Ireland 18–15 at Lansdowne Road in a match to commemorate 80 years of the Irish RFU. Irish official Jack Siggins, who had been the Lions tour manager, had a consoling word for him. "We missed you in South Africa, Garfield," he said.

34

# 4. More success with Wales

Garfield's two-year teacher training course at Shoreditch had ended in the summer of 1955, but he now had thoughts of becoming a PT and games teacher. A specialist qualification, though not an essential requirement, would stand him in good stead and prolong his student days. He was given interviews at the top colleges in this field, Carnegie and Loughborough, preferred the former and enrolled for a one-year course to study for a diploma in physical education in Leeds. The college later merged with Leeds Polytechnic and, in due course, became Leeds Metropolitan University, the Carnegie name surviving as its sports faculty, and as a sponsor of both rugby codes. In 2007 Carnegie became sponsors of the Rugby League Challenge Cup, and in 2008 backed Halifax's match against Australian champions Melbourne.

The course at Carnegie was a way of continuing his sporting lifestyle, but it involved moving to the north of England. He would be unavailable for Newport, so to keep himself fit trained with a local association football team, but played a temporarily farewell game for Newport against an East Monmouthshire XV in a pre-season warm-up game at the beginning of September. He was repeatedly up with the attack and in the dying minutes crossed the line, only for the try to be disallowed for a forward pass from centre Harry Morgan.

Newport were delighted with his form and prevailed upon him to play in the first official fixture of the season against Bristol on Saturday 10 September, before he left for Leeds on the Monday. He was pleased to turn out, but Newport lost 11–6.

A couple of club sides in Yorkshire approached him, but he chose to join the successful Carnegie College side. It turned out to be a sensible decision, not merely from a playing point of view, for there was also an enjoyable social side. As at Shoreditch, there was an interesting mix of younger students fresh from school and older guys from industry wanting to change to teaching. The players would meet together in the pubs in Headingley, generally the New Inn on Otley Road. While the drinking was not really in Garfield's line, there was much singing and a tremendous atmosphere. Leeds was in the rugby league heartlands, but colleges, like universities, the armed forces and other institutions, banned league and only allowed union. He would have chosen union anyway, probably like most of the other students.

Scrum-half Eddie Deasey, a Rochdale boy who later played for Rochdale RUFC and Lancashire, remembers that there was no league influence at all and no real mention of it. Deasey was sometimes the only non-Welshman in a back section that included such as Gethin Evans, who was later to join Newport, though there was another scrum-half, Bernard Bellwood, who played for Harrogate. Captain was second-row forward Ken Carr (or K.W.R. Carr to give him his rugby union title), a former prisoner of war from Birkenhead Park RUFC, who had played many times for Cheshire. He was a disciplinarian who, in the absence of any sort of coach, ran the team.

They played against some of the local club sides, but more often against other colleges, on Wednesday and Saturday afternoons, the Wednesday fixtures following their timetabled gymnastics and swimming sessions in the morning. Most of them were won; the programme for the match against Harrogate at The County Ground on 11 February 1956 gave their playing record so far as played 14, won 12, drawn 1, lost 1, points for 207, points against 89. "Their record does not in itself prove a great deal because their fixture list is not a strong one," explained the accompanying notes, "but it might well have been just as good had they played only leading clubs. Garfield Owen, whom many of us saw on television play such a good game for Wales against Scotland last week, is at full-back."

The lack of first-class opposition was something of a risk for his developing rugby union career, but Garfield did not think it would take the edge off his game. His experience was that a full-back was called upon to work much harder in minor rugby, and there were the Welsh trials to look forward to, in defence of his international full-back berth. He did in fact play three further games for Newport that season, when home for college holidays. The team was even stronger in 1955–56, winning the unofficial Welsh club championship. Garfield appeared

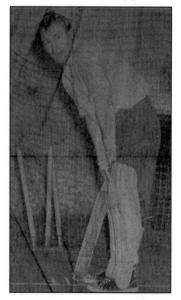

against Watsonians on Boxing Day, and against Neath and Devonport Services at Easter. His plan worked out, the trials – he played in the first and third – were again a success for him, and he retained his place at full-back for Wales.

The news of his selection was broken to him by the local Leeds press, who came searching for him at Carnegie. Being nowhere to be found, they asked where he might be and were directed to the cricket nets at Headingley. The photograph in the following evening's newspaper was of the Welsh international full-back in cricket pads and white shirt.

Garfield knew all about injuries with his experiences the previous season, but still chose to play for Carnegie on

Wednesday afternoon before rushing off to the international on Friday. Other than the traditional late Friday afternoon practice, there were still no other get-togethers before the matches – very different to the situation today. "The game was so much less sophisticated," wrote Welsh star Cliff Morgan in his autobiography. "The truth is that I played mostly off the top of my head. I played it as it happened. This would be unacceptable these days but I don't think was wrong for the 1950s."

He added: "To me, the 1950s was a terrific period for those with talent, who played the game without putting too much thought into it... We just relied on individuals to add extra touches to a pretty basic pattern of play."

The 1956 Five Nations Championship began for Wales with a trip to Twickenham to play England on 21 January. Twickenham held no fears for Garfield, because he had played there the previous season against Harlequins, who used the ground before acquiring The Stoop. He had converted three of Newport's four tries in a 21–0 victory, and taken away memories of the individual baths in the changing rooms, the like of which he had not seen at a ground before. Welsh hopes were high after the forwards' performances in South Africa and under the captaincy of tour star Cliff Morgan, yet it was England who dominated much of the game, watched by a huge crowd of 75,000. They threw away many chances though, and Wales took both of theirs to register tries from Lynn Davies and Russell Robins, Garfield confidently converting the first.

"His conversion of the first try was beautifully kicked from a wide angle," reported *The Times*. Fenwick Allison landed a penalty for England, but missed another from in front of the posts as the match finished 8–3 to Wales. "Only four Welshmen came out of the game with reputations enhanced," wrote Jack Davis in the *Argus*, "Garfield Owen, at full-back, and three of the threequarters. Owen's supreme self-confidence sometimes traps him into unduly delaying a kick, and this happened in the first few minutes, when Jackson charged a kick and Cliff Morgan had to run back to clear. After that Owen played superbly, his instinctive positioning and sure catching countered all England's kicks-on, and his steady kicking helped greatly to keep the English forwards in check."

*The Times* noted that "Both full-backs had a good deal to do under pressure, and it would have been surprising indeed if they had not made a mistake or two. Owen, however, was neatness itself and nearly always perfectly positioned for the catch." And Haydn Tanner concluded that "Garfield Owen had an excellent game at full-back." He "was continually positioning himself brilliantly for Mike Smith's kicks

Wales versus England at Twickenham, 1956. Back: R. Mitchell (referee),
G.D. Owen, M.C. Thomas, R. Robins, R.H. Williams, W.O. Williams,
L.H. Jenkins, I. Jones touch judge); middle: C.C. Meredith, R.C.C. Thomas,
B. Meredith, C.I. Morgan, B.H. Sparks, C.L. Davies, K. Jones;
front: D.O. Brace, H. Morgan.

Garfield converts the first Welsh try in the victory over England
at Twickenham in January 1956. The placer is Onllwyn Brace.

Wales versus Scotland at Cardiff, 1956. Back: I. Jones (WRU), K.J. Jones, T.R. Prosser, J.R.G. Stephens, R.H. Williams, L.H. Jenkins, B. Sparks, L.M. Boundy (referee); middle: B.V. Meredith, R.C.C. Thomas, C.I. Morgan, M.C. Thomas, W.O.G. Williams; front: G. Owen, D.O. Brace, H.P. Morgan, C.L. Davies.

Action from Ireland versus Wales at Lansdowne Road, March 1956. Garfield (right) helps stop Sean Quinlan.

ahead and was finding a long touch in reply, and was steady as a rock at all times." Heady stuff.

The after-match dinner was at the Mayfair Hotel in the West End. The team bus took the players back to the hotel where they were staying, for them to change and make their own way to the nearby Mayfair. Then, while the bus set off for Wales on the Sunday, it was back on the train to Carnegie for Garfield.

Scotland were next up at Cardiff Arms Park on 4 February, the match only saved from the severe frost by volunteers manning braziers dotted around the pitch throughout the night. Wales won 9–3. *Sunday Express* writer G.V. Wynne-Jones was impressed by the Welsh performance on a rock-hard pitch. "Most people thought the treacherous ground would prevent good football," he wrote. "We got more than a good game; we had a near-great one in which the Welsh team were almost always predominant."

Cliff Morgan, Harry Morgan and Lynn Davies scored tries, with Garfield unable to convert the first two and Malcolm Thomas taking over the goalkicking to miss the last. Although his goalkicking was awry, the rest of his game remained of the highest order. Wynne-Jones added that he was "showing superb form on this difficult day at full-back", while J.B.G. Thomas in the *Western Mail* commented: "Behind them all was Garfield Owen, playing his best match for Wales and improving with every kick to give an immaculate display. His skill and accuracy played an important part in meeting the challenge of the fiery Scottish pack, chasing high kicks up field," and "three of his tackles saved certain tries." Jack Davis decided that Garfield had proved that "he is now by a wide margin the soundest full-back in the game. The conditions were almost frightening for full-backs, especially as Scotland were so fond of the old up and under tactics whenever they had the chance, yet it is an astonishing fact that Owen did not miss a single catch. And his touch finding was superb."

With thoughts of a Triple Crown and the Championship, Wales travelled to Lansdowne Road, Dublin on 10 March to play Ireland. Future Welsh legend Gareth Edwards was a young boy aged eight, just beginning to sit up and take notice of rugby because Wales had become a team of which to be proud. He later wrote in his book *Rugby* that he had "discovered this new toy that my parents enjoyed so much, the wireless, and sat with the rest of my family to hear Geevers (the great commentator G.V. Wynne-Jones) describe what I thought would be a mere formality, a Welsh win by lots of points." Things did not go to plan. Ireland moved ahead, "although Wales had scored through a Garfield Owen penalty. I went outside to relieve my nerves by kicking a ball about, confident that when I returned to the house Geevers would be describing the final scenes of a Welsh victory."

He heard instead the cheers accompanying an Irish try, which sealed his heroes' fate. Gareth Edwards later named his first son Owen; he once told Marlene when they were sitting together at a dinner, admittedly with a typical Welsh charmer's twinkle in his eye, that it was after Garfield.

"Welsh hopes of winning their third post-war Triple Crown caved-in during the second half of today's deciding game," reported Dave Phillips in the *South Wales Football Echo*. "Garfield Owen, who played a heroic game, put Wales ahead just before half-time with a magnificent 40-yard penalty goal. But the Irish tide could not be turned and after the interval they overran Wales to the tune of 11 points to 3." It had been a rare mistake by Garfield which had provided the opportunity for the equalising score when, from a mark on his own line, his muffed screw-kick to touch swung back into play to Jack Kyle, who dropped a goal.

The match in the brilliant spring sunshine was no classic as the Welsh went home dejected, Garfield with the small consolation that "if it were not for his cool-as-a-cucumber defence the score against Wales would have been even greater". He was, according to Jack Davis, "the only Welshman to come out of the game with any sort of credit." Dennis Busher added that full-back was the one position where Wales had the edge; "his judgement and fielding as Henderson probed for Welsh defensive weaknesses with high wind-held kicks ahead were magnificent, and his scoring penalty kick could have illustrated the coaching manual". J.B.G. Thomas in the *Western Mail & South Wales News* said, "Rarely, if ever, have I seen a better display of the art of full-back play than that produced by Owen in this match. He was superb."

Dinner afterwards this time was at The Hall on Merrion Row in Dublin, followed by an invitation to a dance organised by Palmerston Football Club, one of the oldest rugby clubs in Ireland, in the Metropole Ballroom, a historic venue and symbol of old Dublin known as the Met, now gone.

Although Gareth Edwards, and millions of others, listened on the radio, the matches were also on the new phenomenon television, helping raise the profile of the players. The black-and-white sets, with their small screens and fuzzy pictures, had risen in prominence following the 1953 Coronation and Wembley FA Cup Final. At first they were expensive and out of reach for many – those who owned or rented them suddenly becoming very popular with the neighbours – but the 1950s were developing into much more prosperous times; between 1952 and 1963 the number of homes with televisions increased from 11 per cent to 85 per cent.

The final match at home to France was the championship decider. There had been many calls for team changes after the performance against Ireland. "Returning home, there was much talk about sacking the lot bar one – Owen," wrote Jack Davis. And changes there were, seven in total, with only Bryn Meredith and Rees Stephens surviving in the pack. A French try put them in front and Wales were heading for defeat until a late controversial score. The French believed that Derek Williams was over the dead-ball line when he grounded a bouncing cross-kick, but the try stood, and Garfield was easily able to add the goal points from beneath the posts to win the match. Reporter H.B. Toft believed that the outstanding players of the match were the two full-backs, Owen and Vannier. "Both made a couple of slips with a very lively ball, but since each was handling oftener than the centres the failures were negligible. Their fielding and kicking alone made this an international match worthy of the name." Wales had won by the skin of their teeth, their third victory from the four matches, making them the outright championship winners.

Events were to conspire to make the France game, his sixth international, Garfield's last. He was invited to represent the Barbarians again on their Easter tour, played for Rees Stephens's International XV against Neath in a fundraiser for the Neath branch of the YMCA, and would seem to have been set for a long stint in the Welsh jersey, with pundits quick to praise his performances. Dave Phillips wrote that the "short, thick-set Owen was considered one of the best full-backs produced by Wales in recent years," while BBC television touted him as "the best full-back in the four countries". J.B.G. Thomas, who in one of his many books was later to select him as the best Welsh full-back since the Second World War, wrote in the *Western Mail* in September 1956: "Reigning Welsh full-back Garfield Owen gave some memorable performances last season. At Twickenham and Cardiff he showed an almost uncanny sense of position and accuracy of kick. Against France in 1955 he placed a couple of remarkable penalties to show his all-round quality. Like the great players before him, he possesses that coolness and judgment necessary for success in the highest circles. He has many rivals this season; players of quality in Morgan, Davies and Priday, but he has that indefinable something which puts him out in front."

The fact that the Wales team fell from grace would not have helped him had his international union career continued – unless his presence could have arrested that decline. The years between 1957 and 1962 were among the least productive in the history of Welsh rugby. They failed to score in their next match, a 3–0 defeat to England in Cardiff, and scored no tries in the next three consecutive matches, as they slid

42

down the rankings. It was unintentionally a good time to bow out, allowing him to end on a positive note.

Accolades followed in subsequent years. Brian Hodgson, the 15-times Wales full-back of the 1960s, when asked by the *South Wales Echo* (18 November 1972) to pick a team of the best players he had seen or played against, named Garfield as his last line of defence. Then, in the run-up to the Welsh Rugby Union centenary in 1981, the same newspaper launched its own Hall of Fame. They began it on 16 September 1980 with 20 names, a further 10 to be announced each month throughout the season. The 20 included Gareth Edwards, Barry John, Mervyn Davies... and Garfield Owen. "He won only six Welsh caps," it cited, "but his performances for Newport and that brief career in the national side left Garfield Owen established as one of the best full-backs of the lot."

He did not actually get the "six Welsh caps" referred to, for players are only awarded the one. What he did receive were the number 1 shirts. The first of these, from the match against Ireland, he kept, along with the cap. Another he exchanged for an England shirt. Opponents often preferred not to swap; either they wanted it for themselves, or they had already promised it to others. The only England player who would exchange with him was Donald Sanders, the prop forward. Sanders had been in the thick of the action and the sewn-on England badge on his number 8 shirt had annoyingly become torn. Later Sanders became an England selector and Garfield contacted him to see if he could find a replacement. "You've asked at the right time," he said, "I've got one right here in my desk. But don't tell anyone where you got it from." And he hasn't, until now.

The others all found new homes. One went to a Carnegie College friend, who wanted it for his son, another to Ireland full-back Paddy Berkery in exchange for not his Irish shirt, but a vest, and the one from his final match was swapped for wingman Lucien Roge's number 14 France shirt, the French using the modern rugby union numbering system with the full-back being No.15, as did Ireland.

An early one had gone to Islwyn Davies, a supporter from Llanharan known as the 'Memory Man'. Islwyn was not a supporter of the team, but of Garfield. In his early career Davies had followed him around. When Garfield went to Shoreditch, he found himself a job in London to be there for the matches, and when he moved to Carnegie, the guy got a job at a cinema in Leeds. He pestered Garfield for the jersey and he handed it over. "I was holding your jersey last night, and I was floating," he said the next day. In retrospect Garfield wished he had given that one to his dad, but his fan later donated it to Llanharan RUFC, which is what his father would have done, so things turned out well.

While studying at Carnegie, Garfield found time to watch occasional rugby league matches at nearby Headingley, home of test match cricket, Yorkshire CCC and the famous Leeds RLFC. The matches were entertaining, had a good atmosphere, and he had heard the players were well paid.

At home in Llanharan for the holidays, he sought out a couple of former rugby league players, Eynon Hawkins and Idris Towill, to find out more. He knew that Llanharan-born Hawkins had played for Salford and Rochdale Hornets, and internationally for the Welsh rugby league team, but had now returned to the valleys, while he knew that Towill, who lived nearby in Bridgend Road, had played for Huddersfield before the war. In fact Towill had done much more than merely play for Huddersfield – as a centre he had scored a try for them at Wembley in their 1935 Challenge Cup Final defeat against Castleford, had been back to Wembley two years later with Keighley, where in 1946 he was awarded a benefit match, and like Hawkins had won international honours for Wales. Towill offered to call round to chat to him, and knocked on the door one evening. His father answered and did not want to let him in, not because he considered Towill a leper because he had played rugby league, but because someone might see and think his son was talking of turning professional. That would have caused problems as well as reducing Garfield's future possible bargaining power. Garfield talked him round, aided by his mother who said she was not leaving any visitor standing on the doorstep, and he got the information and encouragement he needed.

Garfield's life was about to take a dramatic turn.

# 5. Turning professional

Garfield's plan for 1956–57 was to rejoin Newport, find a teaching post, and get married to Marlene. The first two were not to prove straightforward. He had played only four games for Newport the previous season with his Wales and Carnegie commitments, which had allowed his full-back position to be taken by Norman Morgan, whose goalkicking had set a new club record of 159 points in a season. Morgan went on to make 210 appearances for Newport and win international honours himself. Garfield was selected for the first game of 1956–57 against Penarth, but in attempting a long-range kick at goal he pulled a muscle in his thigh. "I hadn't warmed up properly," he admits. He carried on and Newport won 11–3, despite the team not playing well. "The pack and Garfield Owen, his old calm and efficient self, were the only sections of the team to come out with any sort of credit," wrote the *South Wales Argus*. However, the injury forced him out of action and enabled Morgan to regain his place. He attempted a comeback with the reserve team, Newport United, at Talywain a couple of weeks later, but aggravated the injury and faced more appearances with the second team when he was fit again.

No job was in the offing either. The process was to apply to education authorities rather than schools directly, his native Glamorgan being his first port of call. Cowbridge Grammar School would have been ideal, but nothing was offered by them, or any other school. The Newport club used their contacts to put his name round Monmouthshire, including Newport High School where team-mate Ken Jones had a post, but again no interview was forthcoming.

It was at this point that *The Daily Herald* printed a piece of rugby league gossip saying "Halifax offer Owen £5,000". This was a phenomenal amount of money, for in 1956 the average house price in the UK was £2,280. Inflation in other sectors has been rather less than housing since then, so a figure of around £95,000 might be a reasonable estimate of its current value. The newspaper story was untrue, for he had never spoken to Halifax or any other rugby league club, but it was intriguing. He had already thought about rugby league, and this made him think about it a bit harder. His wedding to Marlene was only six months away and the money would be more than useful.

Rugby league at Halifax's level was a professional sport – or semi-professional because players usually also had jobs away from the game. Unlike at Newport, where he could claim only expenses, albeit admittedly handsome, at Halifax there would be match pay as well as the signing-on fee. He therefore decided to telephone the Halifax club to ask them about it. On the other end of the line he heard a familiar Welsh accent, for Halifax's secretary-manager was Bill Hughes, a native of South Wales. Hughes told him that he knew nothing about the newspaper story either, but took the opportunity to inquire if he would have been interested if it had been true. Garfield replied that he might well be. He knew the town, having visited with a group from Carnegie to witness the schools' PE programme, which was highly regarded and known for good practice. It seemed a promising place to find work.

Halifax were one of the leading rugby league clubs at the time, having been a major force through the 1950s, with attendances at Thrum Hall generally hovering around the 10,000 mark. They had appeared in the showpiece Challenge Cup Final at Wembley three times in the last seven years, being runners-up to Bradford Northern in 1949, drawing with Warrington before missing out in the famous replay at Odsal Stadium in 1954, and then losing again to St Helens the previous April. They had been beaten Championship finalists in 1952–53, 1953–54 and 1955–56 and had generally dominated the game east of the Pennines, winning the Yorkshire League on four occasions and the Yorkshire Cup twice.

The team was built on great forwards, including Jack Wilkinson, Alvin Ackerley, John Thorley, John Henderson, Les Pearce, Derrick Schofield, Albert Fearnley and Ken Traill. They also had stars behind the pack in half-backs Ken Dean and Stan Kielty, threequarters Tommy Lynch, Geoff Palmer, Dai Bevan and Arthur Daniels and a renowned full-back in Tuss Griffiths. The last four seasons had seen them finish the league season in second-place in 1952–53, top in 1953–54, fourth in 1954–55 and second behind Warrington in 1955–56.

Longstanding full-back Griffiths, himself a Welshman and former Newport player back in season 1945–46, had signed from Doncaster in 1952 and kicked 438 goals in 151 matches, including a record 147 in the last season. However, like some of the other players, age was catching up with him and he was past his best. He had played his last game for Halifax in September and moved on to Dewsbury. The club had a ready-made replacement in Peter 'Billy' Briers, a former Castleford amateur rugby league player, but a big-name full-back was on the club's shopping list.

Being a limited company like many league clubs, Halifax were run by a board of directors. Usually in the 1950s this comprised nine local businessmen, most of them willing to put in a bit of cash when needed to help the club along. Fans were quick to criticise them if things were not perfect on the field, which seemed to be the case in 1956. The team had won seven of its 11 games since the start of the season in August, and reached the semi-final of the Yorkshire Cup only to bow

46

out narrowly at Wakefield, but expectations were huge. As supporters themselves, the directors knew that the team needed a new big name — what would now be called a marquee signing — to replace aging and departed players.

Tommy Lynch, a former New Zealand All Black rugby union star, had completed four magnificent seasons in the centre, but a serious eye injury had forced him out of the game four months ahead of his scheduled return home in December on completion of his contract. Winger Dai Bevan had also just retired. The directors made efforts to sign international second-row forward Geoff Gunney, but his club Hunslet had given them short shrift, as often happened. Turning to rugby union would avoid that, because the player's club would not need to approve the signing, so from the directors' viewpoint the news of Garfield's interest was opportune; he was just the player they needed to replace Tuss Griffiths. From Garfield's perspective, like so often before in his life, he would be going where he was wanted.

Throughout their history Halifax had looked to Wales to sign players, from internationals to promising juniors. Modern times have seen most clubs turn to Australians, New Zealanders and South Sea Islanders to bolster their ranks, Halifax being well to the forefront, but previously the hunting ground to supplement the home-grown talent was Wales. At the time, the Rugby League International Board had imposed a ban on recruiting players from Australia and New Zealand anyway, to protect the leagues in those countries, so such attractions were out of reach.

Clubs like Halifax would often employ talent scouts in Wales to seek out the best prospects, though they did not always need to, sometimes being contacted by locals who took on the role of modern-day agents, touting potential targets around various league clubs in search of the best deal, for themselves probably more than the player because they would be in for a cut. The best value for these clubs would be young players whose signing-on fees would not be too great, like a Johnny Freeman or Colin Dixon, who were not union internationals. There was no weekly wage for them, but instead payment by results. Winning pay at Halifax was normally £9 before tax in the mid-1950s (equal to about £170 in 2011), with around half of that for a defeat. This was when the average weekly pay for a skilled man was about £11 and an unskilled man £7. Players earning both would be relatively well off, and the Halifax directors were usually able to find work for the incoming recruits. In full-time professional association football, a maximum wage was in operation, set in 1956 at £15 a week, so a rugby league player with a decent job stood to earn more than a top footballer such as Stanley Matthews. The RFL's Management Committee had made its own moves towards a maximum wage rule in 1955, recommending £8 winning pay. At an Extraordinary General Meeting the clubs had voted 17–12 in favour, but that was less than the required two-thirds majority and the idea was eventually dropped.

As long ago as 1891, before the split of 1895, Halifax had acquired a Welsh centre named Bill Keepings from Cardiff, and since then had rarely fielded a team without at least one Welshman. Some failed to make the grade, but others figure prominently in the club's history. In the years before the First World War came Wax Williams (Cardiff), Billy Williams (Pontypool), Tommy Grey (Swansea), Stuart Prosser (Pontypool), Bobbie Lloyd (Pontypool) and Jack Beames (Newport). In the 1920s and 1930s Welsh players included Dai Rees (Abertillery), Eddie Watkins (Neath), Candy Evans (Pontypool), Dick Davies (Swansea), George Baynham (Pontypool), Mel Meek (Newport), Arthur Childs (Cross Keys), Jim Bevan (Cwmavon) and Arthur Bassett (Cardiff). The 1940s and 1950s had brought Mike Condon (Swansea), Terry Cook (Cardiff) and Gwilym Bowen (Swansea), while the current squad included mighty prop John Thorley (Neath), speedy wingers Arthur Daniels (Llanelli) and Johnny Freeman (Cardiff International Athletic Club), and powerhouse second-rower Les Pearce (Swansea), later to become a successful coach and to take charge of Wales in the 1975 World Cup. Lots of others turned down their approaches, not least of whom was one dubbed by the press as the "golden boy of Welsh rugby", Lewis Jones. The club minutes record that in September 1951 a deputation travelled to South Wales with a mandate to sign him, but their offer was rejected. Many other rugby league clubs used the same tactics, all helping to make them most unwelcome in Wales among club officials and supporters, if less so with the players.

Negotiations with Garfield were quickly in place. Halifax offered the services of the club solicitor to speed things up, but he was too canny for that. He engaged a friend of his fiancée's father to act on his behalf when the parties met at the Queen's Hotel in Manchester (now the Hotel International) across the street from Piccadilly train station, on the afternoon of Wednesday 17 October 1956. Halifax's representatives were Welshman Bill Hughes and directors Selwyn Heppenstall and Ted Horsfall, who were almost at their wits' end by the time Garfield's solicitor had gone through the contract verbatim. The appointment had to be kept a complete secret in Wales, for had it been known about he would have been banned from rugby union — speaking with rugby league clubs was taboo under union's strict rules on professionalism — and his negotiating powers with Halifax considerably reduced. He was unable even to tell his father, a source of much regret, or his friends and team-mates at Newport, Maesteg and Llanharan. He did manage to talk it through with Marlene though, cadging a lift on the Newport team bus during his injury spell to their match at Blackheath on 13 October. The *South Wales Argus* reported this with suspicion, the day after his signing for Halifax. "Owen, at his own request, travelled to Blackheath on Saturday with the Newport team, though not chosen to play, as he wished to visit his fiancée in Surrey. He did not return with the team." Their mistaken implication seemed to be that he was going off with rugby league agents.

Some of those he was unable to tell might not have been too impressed; many would have had a caricature view of the north of England as a grimy, sooty wasteland populated by cloth-capped Neanderthals indulging in a violent game more like mud-wrestling than rugger, and would not have understood his motives. "You'd get murdered," one had said to him when he mentioned rugby league, but he knew he wouldn't — he had watched the game.

Rugby union administrators in particular regarded those who took the money to play league with revulsion. They could see no hypocrisy in the fact that they took huge sums at the gate, yet expected the players to turn out for nothing and resented those who chose to better themselves financially. It might have been accepted with a stiff upper lip, but "going north" was seen as treason in Wales then. However, although supporters regretted the huge loss of talent to rugby league, the local papers often reported on the progress of their former players in the north. And on occasions the Welsh rugby league team, usually made up of former union players, could attract large crowds.

Although top-level rugby league was semi-professional, even in the early 1950s when interest was at its height after the War years and crowds at their highest, the clubs had little money to throw around. Halifax had recorded a seasonal profit of £3,136 in the 1955–56 Wembley season, but that was exceptional, with the Government's Entertainment Tax taking a 10 per cent slice of gate receipts between 1952 and 1957. Crowds were high, but admission was only two shillings, less than the cost of 10 cigarettes or two pints of beer.

The £5,000 figure for Garfield which had originally been bandied about in the press would have been too high even for a club that had enjoyed the success of Halifax, and would have equalled the rugby league record transfer fee, set in the 1950–51 season when hooker Joe Egan moved from Wigan to Leigh and forward Harry Street from Dewsbury to Wigan. Financial details for players joining from rugby union tended to be less clear-cut and less open. Lewis Jones, finally yielding to pressure and agreeing a deal with Leeds in 1952 to become the most recent big-name Welsh convert, had reportedly received £5,725. For the clubs, there were obvious dangers of paying a big fee up front; the preference was for the money to be spread over a period of time and also dependent on successful performance.

Above: Caricaturist Ken Adams of the *Halifax Courier* illustrates Garfield's signing by Halifax in 1956.

Left: Signing the contract live on the BBC television *Sportsview* programme.

According to the Halifax club minutes, the initial down-payment eventually agreed with Garfield was £1,500, with guarantees of a further £1,075 in stages over the following months. Two additions to the deal which his solicitor was able to secure related to tax and to any future transfer. It was agreed that should Garfield ever be transferred to another club, he would be entitled to 10 per cent of the fee from Halifax, and a further 10 per cent from the receiving club. Additionally, there was discussion at the time that signing fees might lose their tax-free status. The parties agreed that the money for this tax, should be set to one side, and if it was not needed for the government then it would go to Garfield, which is what eventually happened. Despite the presence of solicitors, other promises were verbal rather than written, and dependent to some extent on the directors who made them remaining with the club. Halifax proved to be honourable in this, however, and over time Garfield ended up with not far short of the £5,000 originally mentioned. Also into the bargaining came the matter of jobs, the club agreeing to help find teaching posts for both Garfield and prospective wife Marlene – not that Marlene would ever need any help finding work with her high-level maths qualification.

After six hours of talks the deal was ready to be signed. This was an important publicity moment for Halifax, who had already invited the national press to the Queen's Hotel in Leeds. One of the reporters was Eddie Waring of the *Sunday Pictorial*, which later became the *Sunday Mirror*. Eddie was also the BBC's rugby league commentator, having covered internationals and Challenge Cup Finals in the days before the game became a regular television sport. That began in 1958 and ultimately turned him into a cult figure.

Eddie sensed an opportunity, quite possibly to further his own career, and phoned the BBC, asking to speak to Peter Dimmock personally. Dimmock was head of outside broadcasts and, since 1954 had hosted a Wednesday evening sports news programme *Sportsview*, which became *Sportsnight* in 1968, filmed at Broadcasting House in nearby Oxford Road. With the programme about to go on air, Waring pointed out the significance of the news he was bringing, and insisted that it should be screened live. "This had better be good, Eddie," said Dimmock, who agreed to his programme being interrupted. Less than an hour later Garfield was being interviewed in the studio. He never disputed that money was the reason for the move, as everyone knew that was the case.

Back at the New Inn in Headingley, his former Carnegie team-mates added a new verse to one of the rugby songs in their repertoire, *Did you ever see such a funny thing before?* Sung with a Welsh accent, it went:

They say that Garfield Owen
To the rugby league is going.
Some say that he is crackers,
But he wants the bloody ackers.

Did you ever see,
Did you ever see,
Did you ever see,
Such a funny thing before?

So it was that Garfield became the first rugby player to have the signing away of his amateur status shown live on television. *Sportsview* would not have attracted as many viewers as the leading shows of 1956, *The Gang Show, Armchair Theatre* and *Take your Pick*, but the number of televisions was increasing rapidly and it would have been seen by millions. That did not include his father, who still knew nothing about the day's events until Thursday's newspapers came out, but would have included some of the Newport players, officials and supporters, to whom it must have been a great shock.

When he had failed to turn up for training that Wednesday night, a Newport official had arranged to travel to his home the next day to find out what had happened, but now he knew. Secretary Bill Everson, himself a former Welsh international full-back, said in the press: "I'm surprised. Although it will be a big blow to Newport and Welsh rugby, I hope Owen succeeds up north. I regard him as one of the finest full-backs I have seen. In one way the move is rather lucky — it solves the problem of us having two full-backs, Morgan and Owen, from whom to choose. But we are all very sorry Owen has gone."

The press also reported that before making his decision, Garfield had spoken at length with Lewis Jones about the transition to rugby league. This was not the case, though he was aware that many other players had made the same move and been successful, including some from Newport — the great Trevor Foster of Bradford Northern being one famous example. And of course he remembered his conversations with Idris Towill and Eynon Hawkins. While those two had returned to Wales, most of the others he knew had settled in the north of England, and seemed more than content with their lives there.

Garfield was always confident in his own abilities and felt that he would make a success of rugby league. At 24 years of age, he felt he was young enough and enthusiastic enough to make the transition work. In his view the full-back role was not greatly different, and while he was moving from an amateur sport, many of the games in which he had played had been every bit as serious and tough as rugby league ones would be. A much harder part was leaving Newport, who had

52

been good to him. People there needed to be thanked, but at first he couldn't; to return in the immediate future would have created animosity and just was not possible. "Boats had been burned; sometimes it is just necessary to make a decision about your own life and get on with it," he says.

Penning a deal with Halifax had other repercussions, for he was instantly regarded as a professional in all sports. Not only was he now barred for life from rugby union — or so it seemed at the time — but even more ridiculously it put an end to his athletics career. He had missed qualification for the Welsh javelin team for the 1954 British Empire and Commonwealth Games held in Vancouver, Canada, by six inches. The 1958 Games were to be in Wales, so would have been good to aim for, though now that school and college days were over, opportunities to practise and compete would have been limited. Halifax was not blessed with the greatest athletics facilities in the 1950s.

Garfield immediately moved to Halifax. His wedding was set for the following March, the signing-on fee coming in nicely to pay for the home they would set up thereafter. Until then the club fixed him up with accommodation at The Old Cock Inn on Southgate in the town centre for a night, then at the Golden Lion Hotel at Highroad Well for two more. Following that he moved in with director Ron Marshall at his home in Mytholmroyd for a week, before a more permanent lodging arrangement was made in Warley Road, not far from the Thrum Hall ground, with Mrs Ridsdale and her children Martin and Margaret. It was a good move and he had a fine time there, getting on famously with the whole family. A fond memory is of Sunday lunch. On his first Sunday Mrs Ridsdale bought in a jug of gravy and a great big Yorkshire pudding, and went back to the kitchen. When she returned he hadn't touched it. "What's the matter?" she asked. "I was waiting for the vegetables," he replied. She had to explain that in Yorkshire, a Yorkshire pudding was eaten on its own first.

The club had helped find him a teaching post by arranging an application to the Halifax Education Authority, who then suggested schools. Bolton Brow Junior School was a possibility, but he preferred to work with older pupils, and an offer of a position as a PE teacher at Haugh Shaw Secondary School, which much later merged with Clare Hall to become Halifax High, was more to his liking. The school was undergoing refurbishment at the time though and the gymnasium was not ready, so he spent his first couple of weeks teaching at Ovenden Secondary School. Someone at the Halifax Education Authority must have taken exception to press reports that Garfield was employed by Halifax RLFC, for a notice appeared on the front page of the *Times Educational Supplement* saying that it was they who paid his salary.

Rugby league would still need to be learnt, and there were obstacles to overcome. A big money signing does not always go down well with fellow players who might have signed for a pittance from local amateur clubs, and league supporters can be sceptical that a union player can make it in their perceived tougher game. "You've cost a lot of money," he heard one say. "Make sure you earn it."

The Halifax players were all strangers to him, apart from one whom he knew vaguely. Big Cumbrian centre Geoff Palmer had spent the 1952–53 season with Newport during his National Service, mostly in the second team, Newport United, but once in the first team against Wasps in March. In 1953–54 he had played against Newport when with Rosslyn Park. Brimming with talent, he had signed for Halifax in 1955, been part of the Wembley team in 1956, and settled in the area as a businessman. The pair became good friends.

In Garfield's first training session at Thrum Hall in the near-darkness – just a powerful single light on the side of the pavilion illuminated part of the field in those pre-floodlight days — a player sprinted past him at tremendous speed. "Who was that?" he asked Geoff. "That's Derrick Schofield," came the reply. "He plays in the second-row." It was clear a lot of training would be needed to keep up with these guys.

In charge of the sessions was Frank Dawson, a renowned former Hunslet forward, long referred to by his nickname 'Dolly'. He was an influential leader who had been at the club since 1951; in the traditions of the time he was a trainer rather than a coach, primarily concerned with fitness. His forwards had to be hard and willing to fight, so there was always ample protection for a newcomer.

Garfield was now fully recovered from his early-season injury, having proved his fitness playing for Cliff Morgan's International XV against Bective Rangers to mark the Dublin club's 75th anniversary on 6 October, but could not walk straight into a rugby league match. Halifax's weekend game at home to high-ranking Hull was clearly too soon, though the directors needed him playing as soon as possible to start to get some return on their outlay. "It is not our intention to play Owen at Thrum Hall on Saturday," said football committee chairman Ernest Rushworth in a press interview. "He will watch the game."

It was his first daylight view of the Thrum Hall ground, the corner-to-corner slope on the field being the first thing he noticed, for those at Llanharan, Maesteg and Newport had all been flat. It seemed a peculiar ground in some ways, with nothing particularly encouraging about it; the unique atmosphere and intimacy of the place he discovered later. The main stand compared favourably with Newport, though was smaller in length, the stand opposite was similar, while Thrum Hall had covered terracing behind one set of posts unlike at

Rodney Parade. Some of the standing accommodation was primitive, with the re-terracing of both ends still being a year or two away. He took it as it was though – he just wanted to get on with being a success in his new surroundings.

The directors sitting beside him in the stand made little effort to explain the intricacies of his new sport, but he quickly picked them up for himself. The key things were simple: stop the opposition from scoring, and be in a position to attack if he could. As for the goalkicking, that would be just the same. Rugby league was far less dependent than union on penalty goals, though there were more in the 1950s than today but, to make up for it, there would be significantly more tries than in union from which to attempt conversions.

Halifax, on the back of a 27–6 defeat at league leaders Oldham the previous Saturday, lost the encounter with Hull 14–10, part-time kicker Ken Dean landing two goals. Dean also scored a try, as did Scottish winger Drew Turnbull. They lost the next match as well, at Odsal against Bradford Northern, 17–11. The tricky transitional season was continuing for Halifax after their successes of recent years. The fans were starting to grumble and there was rumour of discontent among the players. Dolly Dawson later seemed to confirm this in his end of season report to the directors when he mentioned "trouble among the forwards", "too much bickering" and "too much losing pay".

Maybe it was not the perfect setting the directors had portrayed, though Tommy Lynch, in a farewell article for the *Halifax Courier* ahead of his return to New Zealand, denied any problems, saying the team had just not clicked yet. There had been some fade outs in the second halves of games, he wrote, but there was no explanation. "No one is more disappointed than the players themselves," he added.

The team needed new blood and Garfield wanted to get into the action, but usually rugby union recruits took time to find their feet. David Watkins, the Newport half-back who followed him into league a decade later, wrote in his autobiography that "one thing I would plead for is an extended period for a rugby union player to be shown patience by league colleagues and fans." He estimated that it took him a full two years to rid himself of the habit of automatically releasing the ball in a tackle.

He was not a full-back, but Gus Risman played there at times when he first turned to league. Risman, another former Welsh union player, had become a legend with Salford, Workington Town and Great Britain in the 1930s and 1940s. In his own autobiography he gave the opinion that it would normally take about three months to adapt. "No matter how good a union player is, it will take him some time before he can fit into a league side," he wrote. It was not just the obvious things like

55

13 players instead of 15, a play-the-ball instead of rucks and mauls, kicks to touch in general play needing to bounce, and the scoring system. To him it was the greater intensity, players needing to be in the thick of the game more, to be faster and fitter. "In fact it might be true to say that only the really star union player – the international – could hold down his place in a league side right from the very start," he wrote.

Well, Garfield was such a player. Frank Williams, sports editor of the local newspaper, the *Halifax Courier*, watched him in training at Thrum Hall and reported that he was in good form, showing fine ability with his kicking to touch, fielding and goalkicking. "Owen appears to be settling remarkably well in his new surroundings, and no one could be more keen to make good." Williams, another Welshman, was a former league international, having taken part in the famous Rorke's Drift test match in Australia on the 1914 tour, so his views tended to be well respected by players and supporters alike.

Garfield's first taste of league was to be the 'A' team game against Bradford, at Thrum Hall on 27 October, at the same time the first team were playing at Odsal. Just 13 players were required for the seniors in these days, plus one or two travelling reserves, so the 'A' team was a strong one, destined to finish fourth in its league, the Yorkshire Senior Competition.

It was not packed with youngsters as modern reserve teams were to become, but included seasoned performers like Billy Mather, who had played in the 1954 Challenge Cup Final replay, and former Dewsbury enforcer Stan Moyser, alongside future favourites John Burnett and Keith Williams, and local stalwarts like Jack Helliwell, David Sykes and John Mitchell. The full Halifax team was: Owen, Asquith, Burnett, Mather, Mitchell, Williams, Richardson, Clegg, Moyser, Helliwell, Wynn, Wagstaff, Sykes.

A bumper crowd of nearly 3,000, around double the normal figure, turned up to see Garfield kick eight goals in a 37–7 victory. The *Halifax Courier* reported that "though the Welshman did nothing spectacular, he showed obvious signs of picking up the threads of the RL game quickly. His positioning was good, he tackled safely and with resolution, while his long-range kicking improved as the game progressed. He landed eight goals and had several near misses. A satisfactory first performance and a happy augury for the future." His debut with the first team could not be far away.

# 6. Starting out at Halifax

In 1956–57 Halifax and Hull, the Championship finalists from the previous season, took part in an International Club Championship with the two leading French sides, Albi and Carcassonne. RC Albi had beaten AS Carcassonne 13–5 in the equivalent French play-off final. It was an attempt to emulate football's European Cup, which had been launched a year earlier for the champions of all the national football leagues. The editor of the French newspaper *L' Equipe* had been a prime mover in persuading UEFA to put it into practice, the newspaper had provided the trophy, and the first European Cup Final had been played at Parc des Princes in Paris in front of 38,239 spectators.

The rugby league version turned out to be much less spectacular and was abandoned after its debut season. The clubs, or certainly Halifax, did not take it too seriously. For the matches against the French sides the Halifax players received just £6, which was normal losing pay, regardless of the result — usual winning pay was £9, with 10 shillings extra for each consecutive win up to a maximum of £15.

Halifax were scheduled to travel to France in November to meet both Albi and Carcassonne, presenting an ideal opportunity to blood their new big rugby union signing. A full-strength squad of 17 players was selected, though not incumbent full-back Peter Briers, and all were to play in at least one of the matches. A plane was chartered to the base at Toulouse, with some spectators being invited to join the trip at a cost of £17 for travel and hotel. The travel agent Thomas Cook's final account was £1,298. This was all familiar territory for Garfield, who had been on tours with Llanharan, Newport and the Barbarians, and to France with Wales. However, he had rarely met anyone quite like Halifax's Johnny Freeman and Drew Turnbull, the team's two pin-up boys, who were out on the town at the first opportunity chasing, and catching, the French girls.

He duly made his Halifax first team debut at Albi's Stade Maurice-Rigaud in the south of France on Thursday 1 November 1956, kicking two goals as Halifax won 19–11. Albi were a strong team with five French internationals, though some were reported to be absent on military service in North Africa. "One of the pleasing features of the match," reported Frank Williams in the *Courier*, "was the promising display of Garfield Owen. The new full-back fielded a greasy ball like an artist, while his goalkicking, although he had near misses, was excellent. Above all, his positional play was outstanding. All he needs is rugby league fitness. Once he attains this he will be a valuable asset. He often linked up cleverly." The Halifax team was Owen,

Turnbull, Mageen, Palmer, Freeman, Dean, Kielty, Thorley, Moyser, Wilkinson, Henderson, Pearce, Traill.

Three days later he kicked three more goals in a 24–9 victory over Carcassonne. It was Halifax's first ever Sunday match; Rugby Football League rules in England prohibited play on the Sabbath. Mather, Broadhurst, Ackerley and Marchant replaced Mageen, Palmer, Pearce and Traill. Loose-forward Jack Marchant was sent off by the French referee, but the players were surprised to see him return to the field five minutes later. The French, much ahead of their time, used the sin bin to punish foul play, and Marchant had unknowingly become the first Halifax player to experience it. Consequently, some of his colleagues, notably explosive hooker Stan Moyser, rubbed their hands at the thought of a sending off being for only five minutes. "Once more Owen gave a grand display at full-back," ran the report. "His fielding was again a feature, his leading up work led to Turnbull's second try, and his last goal was a peach." Drew Turnbull scored three tries in each of the matches.

A pleasant few days in France included a five-hour stay in the ancient town of Albi. Looking round the shops there, he spotted a camera he really liked, but did not have enough money with him — around £25 in English money — to buy it. One of the supporters on the trip, unbeknown to Garfield, bought it and, when back in England sold it to him. There was also a visit to the Mediterranean coast and to the Pyrenees, though several players became ill through drinking Vichy water, a naturally sparkling mineral water, supposedly with positive health benefits. At the end of an eventful trip, there was panic on the return flight when the plane ran low on fuel and had to land at Jersey.

Garfield played in the return match against Albi at Thrum Hall the following April, kicking three goals in a narrow 21–20 success. This time Halifax had another rugby union covert making his debut in scrum-half Bryn Jones, a student at Carnegie. Jones had not been at Carnegie during Garfield's time, but he knew of Jones as a Blackpool-based Lancashire county star and was happy to endorse him to the directors, who saw him as the intended replacement for Stan Kielty. The match turned into a thriller, full-back André Rives having the chance to win the game for the Frenchmen with virtually the last kick of the match. Speedy winger Capu left the "usually brilliant tackler Garfield Owen bewildered on at least two occasions" according to the *Courier*, "Owen having difficulty turning owing to a thigh injury." The injury forced him to make way for Peter Briers against Carcassonne, who were beaten 33–10 two days later. The normal league matches against Hull counted as the other matches in the competition and, since Hull won both, Halifax finished the tournament as runners-up. Attendances had been reasonable — 7,014 and 4,836 for the home games with the French teams, 11,246 and 22,000 for the Hull matches home and away respectively — but while football's European Cup flourished, league's International Club Championship bit the dust.

Garfield's first match in the league was at Salford on Saturday 10 November where, for the only time that season, he failed to score, though Halifax achieved a notable 6–5 victory. Phil King, in *The People* the following day, described the match as "a terrific thrill-packed contest". Garfield, he wrote, "missed four difficult kicks at goal, but looked very sound and was always ready to run with the ball." In Monday's *Daily Mail*, Derek Marshall added: "Garfield Owen missed four goal kicks, and they might have cost his club the match, but his general play was highly encouraging. He tackled well, recovered brilliantly from a shaky start to a touch-finding duel with Gregory, and showed neat timing in linking up with his own threequarters. With more experience he should prove a valuable asset." Frank Williams in the *Halifax Courier* thought "his general play stamped him as a full-back of class, with tackling, catching and positional play almost faultless."

He made his home debut the following Saturday against Leeds. "Garfield Owen with four rugby league games behind him, plays his first senior game at Thrum Hall today," said the match programme. "His progress since joining the professional code from the amateur ranks has been remarkable. We look forward to seeing him in action as our last line of defence for many years to come. We wish him luck and trust that he will be very happy and successful with us at Halifax."

Leeds, flying high in the league table, were beaten 15–11, Garfield landing three goals, as the successful run continued. Colin Clifft, a loose-forward who had been capped by England the previous May, was signed from Wakefield Trinity to add a further boost and, by the time the Challenge Cup came round, Halifax were on a roll. As cup finalists the previous season, they entered the competition with confidence. After a comfortable first round victory over amateur qualifiers Widnes St Maries, they achieved a noteworthy win away to one of the hot favourites, Hull, when both teams scored a try, but Garfield's three goals proved to be the difference. For the third round, the last chance of a home draw before the neutral venue semi-finals, they got their wish, though it was a tough one — Leeds at Thrum Hall.

The league fixture a few weeks earlier had attracted a slightly higher than average crowd of 12,800, but the Challenge Cup was a huge attraction for rugby league fans in the 1950s. The match was made all-ticket, with a limit of 27,500 spectators. Today's safety officers would never have sanctioned such a figure, but it was below the ground record, which had stood at 29,122 since 1913. The tickets sold out in no time, generating receipts of £4,250.

59

Left: Congratulations on a job well done at Salford. Youngsters, and others, always came on to the pitch at the final whistle.

Middle: A break out of defence at Thrum Hall against Widnes, January 1957. Halifax were in a blue shirt change strip. Garfield ran with the ball in rugby league far more often than he remembers. (Photo: *Halifax Courier*)

Bottom: Garfield (right) with Halifax players, officials and guests, grounded in Jersey in 1956.

A Halifax team in 1956–57. Back: John Thorley, Johnny Freeman, Les Pearce, Colin Clifft, Jack Wilkinson, Geoff Palmer; front: Ron Asquith, Garfield Owen, Billy Mather, Ken Dean, Stan Moyser, Stan Kielty. Only 12 players are shown, Ken Traill being late out of the changing rooms. (Photo: *Halifax Courier*)

Following Ken Dean through the crowd down Thrum Hall's historic corner steps on to the field in 1956.

Lewis Jones, by then well established in league at Leeds, said much about the match in his autobiography, including a wish that it could have been switched to "a ground large enough to accommodate a more generous proportion of the thousands so evidently desperate to see". His home and workplace had apparently been besieged during the preceding week by supporters desperate for tickets. Halifax he regarded as the toughest opposition imaginable: "Certainly we would have liked to avoid meeting Halifax until such time as the elimination process offered us no option." Jones was aware that Halifax included five Welshmen in Garfield Owen, Arthur Daniels, Johnny Freeman, John Thorley and Les Pearce, but "Countrymen or not, we never have either time or opportunity for the social graces on these occasions, and this was no exception." He records Leeds being penalised and Garfield kicking a "grand goal from the touchline", and Ken Traill sending the Thrum Hall crowd into ecstasies with two tries, one converted by Garfield. "With only 20 minutes gone," he writes, "our hopes of Wembley were dying."

Not for the only time ever though, Leeds fought back to take the lead, a further late try giving them a 16–10 victory. For Garfield, the players and fans it was a huge disappointment. Instead of Halifax at Wembley, it was Leeds, who went on to beat Whitehaven in the semi-final, then Barrow in the final to win the cup.

In the league competition, the season petered out, Halifax slipping to 12th place of the 30 clubs in the final table. Garfield's record for the season was 91 goals from 31 appearances. He kicked at least one goal in every match he played apart from his first league match of all at Salford, including three goals in a rare 6–3 win against the touring Australians on a Tuesday afternoon in December. Bernard Ingham, then a *Yorkshire Post* reporter before his later incarnation as Prime Minister Margaret Thatcher's chief press secretary, reported that referee John Clapham from Wigan awarded Halifax two penalties in the last 11 minutes for obscure scrum infringements by Australia. "Garfield Owen, whose display at full-back far exceeded the standard expected in view of the heavy ground conditions, cleverly defied a boisterous cross-wind to kick both. His accuracy robbed the Australians of a victory they deserved, if only for the fact that they scored the only try of the game."

Other reports mentioned the novelty of seeing the two full-backs, Garfield and Australia's Clive Churchill, engage in "some old-fashioned long distance kicking." To this day, Halifax have not beaten the Kangaroos since.

Garfield had quickly adapted to his new code, gaining the plaudits of the skipper at the time, Ken Dean. "He had a tough act to follow in Tuss Griffiths," says Ken, "but despite playing behind a lesser team, he succeeded. You always felt safe with him in defence at your back. He was always there, always in the right place."

In fact, he had altered his game little from how he had played rugby union. The goal-kicking and tackling were much the same anyway, but he also continued to use his kicking in general play to good effect. Allan Cave of the *Daily Herald* was impressed. "He takes his goal kicks with his right foot," he noted, "but can use either left or right in clearing kicks." These were the days of unlimited tackles, when teams could potentially hold on to the ball for long spells, so kicking it away was not a common tactic. However, once Dolly Dawson had seen his prodigious boot, he was happy to allow him to kick downfield, either to touch, where unlike in rugby union it would have to bounce in the field of play first, or to an isolated opposition full-back or winger. The offside rules allowed players to be in front of the kicker so long as they stayed 10 yards away from the receiving player. Team mates such as Alvin Ackerley and Jack Wilkinson would call for the kick, then rush to intimidate the catcher from 10 yards away. Sometimes the sledging would encourage him to kick it back, generally less well than Garfield, but if he didn't his team mates would still have to retreat behind him to start advancing all over again. If he was harassed enough to drop it, or indeed if the kick found touch, international hooker Ackerley had all the skills to win the ensuing scrum. Once Ackerley moved on to Hull KR, Halifax were quick to recruit another proven ball-winner in John Shaw, himself a future international.

Being able to use his rugby union skills really helped him to settle. Lewis Jones had found just the same thing when he started in league, also at full-back, similarly belting the ball upfield. "I was at least keeping out of trouble," he wrote. "It saved me making a fool of myself."

Suitably encouraged, Garfield continued to use another rugby union ploy for a while at Halifax — the mark. It was still in the rugby league rule book that a free kick could be claimed after a clean catch of an opposition kick. He had used it regularly as a method of self-preservation in union, where a shout of "Mark!" would stop the onrushing forwards from crashing into him. It was more by instinct than anything else that he tried it in league, though for some reason it did not halt the opposing forwards quite so readily. A problem with it in league was that from the resultant free kick, the ball could not be tapped, but had to be kicked, and only into touch if it bounced first, as in general play, so it had long been disused. On one occasion at Leigh he claimed a mark deep in defence near the left touchline. The Leigh players lining on that side more or less challenged the silly Welsh so-and-so (or words to that effect) to bounce the ball out of play. He had noticed though that the far touchline was unguarded and, knowing he could kick that far, belted the ball off the field on that side instead.

Maurice Bamford, in one of his books of rugby league stories, tells the tale of how a few years later Dewsbury put up a bomb to him. It hung long enough for him to notice his former team-mate Jack Marchant steaming in. "Mark!" Garfield yelled hopefully. "There are no marks anymore," responded Jack as he barrelled into him. He was not correct, since they were not deleted from the rules until 1964, but Garfield was probably the last league player to use them. Even he had rejected them long before 1964.

Something else at which he was quite adept, and not often seen in rugby league, was an ability to stretch out and catch an opposition penalty kick over the touchline, pulling it back into play before it could hit the ground. "His positioning in this respect, as in all others, was immaculate, and his arms were surely telescopic," wrote Robert Gate in *Gone North, (Volume 2)*.

His general positional play, always a strength, needed to change slightly. In rugby union, the backs lined up diagonally, whereas in rugby league they were more likely to run straight at you, making them harder to tackle. In defence, he positioned himself in line with the ball, attempting to always force the attacker out towards the touchline. "I tried to read their body language so I knew what they were planning to do," he remembers. "At times you got caught out, but it usually worked."

The supposedly tougher, more professional, game of league brought its moments of intimidation, but whenever he ran into trouble a forward was always quick to support, more often than not Les Pearce. "Who was it?" he'd ask, with a threatening stare at opponents still in the vicinity. Garfield's own game was more about the sportsmanship with which he had been brought up, never averse to helping injured rivals or acknowledging their talents, much to the disapproval of some of his colleagues.

Among many great wingers to test his defence to the full was Barrow's Frank Castle. In one match at Craven Park, Castle scored five tries, showing such skill for one of them that Garfield could only applaud, as he had always done when witnessing great play. Ultra-professional skipper Ken Traill, to whom winning, or more accurately winning pay, meant everything, was apoplectic. For goalkicks, when conditions allowed, Garfield would dig up the ground with his heel to make a tee then, after the kick, pat the mound back down flat again. This also was not to Traill's liking. "We pay a groundsman to do that," he'd scream. "Get back in position."

Then there were missed goalkicks. At Blackpool Borough in December, new captain Ken Dean kept calling him up to try for the two points, but Garfield repeatedly failed to find the target. "For goodness sake, Ken, you're flogging a dead horse," cried Traill. He did eventually kick five goals to secure a 19–15 win, and newspaper headlines sang his praises, much to Traill's disgust. Yet although they nearly came to blows at times, for Garfield was never one to back down, he respected Ken Traill. "I had a lot of time for him. He let you know if you were not pulling your weight."

Goalkicking when the ground was hard, either through frost in winter or dryness at the beginning and end of the season, could be problematic, for it could be hard to stop the ball falling over. Once at Featherstone he had landed five or six, and the match was as good as won, when he lined up another, again taking some time to place the ball to his liking. A wag in the crowd shouted out, "For Christ's sake, give him the two points and let's get on with the game!"

While he found the game very similar to rugby union, there was a big difference in the social side. It was not so much the drinking, as he had never bothered with alcohol, but more the fun in the clubhouse after the match, which had been something of a tradition in Wales. At league grounds this seemed virtually nonexistent, the only fun being in training if people were messing around. There was a bar in the Thrum Hall pavilion, but it belonged to the cricket club and was not widely used by the rugby players. The Supporters' Club had plans in place for a bar under the main stand, but these never materialised, and an alternative scheme for a bar — later named the Taverner's Bar — in the Newstead corner did not see fruition until after he had left. Even then for many years it was primarily a drinking den for fans, with an uncarpeted concrete floor.

On the international scene, a Rugby League World Cup competition in Australia was fixed for the end of the season, presenting an opportunity for Garfield to make up for missing out on the 1955 rugby union Lions tour. Great Britain were World Cup holders, his fellow Welsh team mate John Thorley having been at prop when they had won the first tournament in 1954, and in 1956 had also won back the Ashes from Australia in convincing fashion, so were pre-tournament favourites. The press began to speculate. "Garfield Owen is killing the old saying that a rugby union player takes virtually a season to get the hang of rugby league football," said one. "His form since he joined Halifax has brought hopes that he may solve our test goalkicking problems. Owen could be in our World Cup team at the end of the season." Allan Cave of *The Daily Herald* was one who continually talked him up, while *Rugby League Gazette* editor Norman Berry observed that "Garfield Owen, only just into rugby league this season, has brought himself into prominence by some scintillating displays."

What he could have done with was a tour trial in which he could outplay the opposition full-back as in his union days but, although rugby league had used trials on occasions, there were none in 1957. The selectors instead observed him playing at Thrum Hall: "Yesterday they watched Garfield Owen of Halifax and liked his form," wrote Eddie Waring in April, adding "A goalkicker MUST go with the team."

The selection process in league was even more cumbersome than in union. It was the responsibility of the Rugby League Council's International Committee, which comprised 13 club representatives. None were from Halifax, so there would be no help there. For Garfield it was not to be, the full-back selection vote going to Glyn Moses of St Helens, like him a former Maesteg player. Moses was not a goal-kicker, but the party included the man who did kick for Saints, Austin Rhodes, plus the prolific Lewis Jones, the game's leading marksman in 1956–57 with 194. Also selected was Geoff Gunney, the forward Halifax had tried to sign from Hunslet. Garfield had to settle for the not inconsiderable honour of being selected as one of six emergency reserves, suggesting that had it been a full tour, with 26 players instead of 18, he would have been included. "The six shadow reserves – Owen, Rollin, Parkinson, Don Robinson, K. Jackson and Smith – will all have to be vaccinated and inoculated ready to step in, in case of late withdrawals," reported Phil King in *The People*. Sadly, from Garfield's point of view, there was to be no emergency, apart from Great Britain failing to deliver and Australia winning the World Cup.

It was unfortunate that in this period there was little other representative rugby available to him. A European Championship involving England, Wales, France and Other Nationalities, a team for countries other than these, had taken place over recent seasons, but had now been discontinued. The rugby league international calendar had traditionally included the Welsh, with matches being played in Wales reasonably regularly despite there being no Welsh club sides. In the late 1940s and early 1950s there had been matches at Swansea and Abertillery, but attendances in Wales had fallen. Wales continued to play until 1953, but then it was decided that a decreasing number of union converts meant that Wales was no longer strong enough to compete. Welsh players were included in the Other Nationalities side in the 1955–56 Championship, which proved to be its last season. The Welsh team was not reformed until 1968, too late for Garfield.

County rugby was not available to him either, selection criteria for Yorkshire, Lancashire and Cumberland in the 1950s requiring that players could only represent their county of birth or the county in which they had first played junior rugby.

# 7. Hiccups, medals and marriage

Halifax improved in 1957–58, which brought a final league position of sixth. The Rugby Football League operated a system of Yorkshire and Lancashire leagues, which ran alongside the normal table, and involved constructing separate standings for matches played only against teams from, in Halifax's case, Yorkshire clubs. Halifax lost only three matches against Yorkshire opposition to carry off the Yorkshire League Championship for the fourth time in six seasons. Garfield thus had his first rugby league medal.

He also had another familiar face as a new playing colleague. The Halifax directors had returned to South Wales to snare Garfield's former school and international team-mate Brian Sparks from Neath. Sparks had won seven Wales rugby union caps as a flanker and was also now about to become a schoolteacher. He had attended St Luke's College, Exeter, and had captained them to victory in the 1957 Middlesex Sevens. Halifax also recruited Wyn Phillips, a young, promising centre who was later to achieve more success in the forwards, from Llanelli, where he had started to carve a name for himself alongside internationals Cyril Davies and Carwyn James.

One of the other heroes of this Halifax team was another Welshman, winger Johnny Freeman, who the previous year had scorched over for a club record 48 tries. In the first 20 matches of this term he added an amazing 38 more, but in that 20th match at Batley on 21 December a serious knee injury put him out of action for the rest of the season. By comparison, Garfield's try total was again zero. Setting off on a run away from supporting players had more or less been drummed out of him in union. Fear of isolation was less of a problem in league, but was still present, and he mostly adopted the same stance, or passed the ball to Johnny Freeman. "I sought the comfort of the touchline," recalls Garfield. "I don't remember running with the ball much."

He did kick 62 goals that season, but only played in 20 of the 41 matches. It was the year in which Prime Minister Harold Macmillan claimed that "Indeed, let us be frank about it — most of our people have never had it so good", but for Garfield it did not feel like that. At the end of October he lost his place to Peter Briers, who as well as being a decent left-footed goalkicker, ran with the ball more than Garfield and had been starring in the 'A' team. In those days the Halifax team, like most others, was selected not by the coach, but by the board of directors. Club policy was to nominate four members of the board to serve on a Football Sub-committee, who would get together prior to every board meeting and deal with all matters concerning the football side of the club, including recommending the teams to play in each match. Those recommendations were then placed before the full board for their confirmation. "In nine cases out of 10 the recommendations of the Football Sub-committee are approved," said a statement in a later club programme. The training staff would be informed of the requirements, "and then left completely in charge of training on the field".

It was very much the case that the board was paying the wages, so they picked the team, even though at times their knowledge of the game was limited. The sub-committee at this time comprised Selwyn Heppenstall, Ernest Rushworth, Harold Webster and Bill Chalcraft, keen supporters and long-standing directors, but not former players.

Halifax were now trying to adopt a more attacking and adventurous game, with less use of kicking in general play, which reduced Garfield's effectiveness. There was still his great tackling skill and prolific goalkicking, though even the latter deserted him in a match against Bradford Northern. Halifax had won 16–8, but during the game the goalkicking duties had been taken over by a newly-arrived young Scottish forward called Charlie Renilson. Renilson would develop into another great star, though not as a goalkicker. The Football Sub-committee, with Lower Market trader Selwyn Heppenstall to the fore, decided that Garfield was out of form, and should spend some time in the second team. It was all down to his recent marriage they said; it often happened, newly married men were only interested in one thing and it wasn't rugby. As well as his goalkicking, they also found fault with his defence, a criticism that was a particular annoyance, for his tackling was clearly one of his strengths. To miss a tackle on someone like Billy Boston, Tom van Vollenhoven or Frank Castle did not mean he could no longer defend. Many wingers possessed notable evasive skills, while Boston in particular was a fearsome opponent, virtually impossible to halt front-on.

Selwyn Heppenstall was never Garfield's favourite. He once called a meeting to discuss the team's indifferent from. In criticising Brian Sparks and Jack Wilkinson, veteran of bruising Great Britain versus Australia test matches, for dropping the ball in the tackle, he suggested it was because they were trying to protect themselves and must be soft. There were not many people who would dream of calling either of these two soft, and Garfield voiced his disapproval.

If indeed he had lost his touch, which he disputed, it was more likely down to what would now be called second-season syndrome than to Heppenstall's marriage theory – something he had never really had to contend with in his union career. Opponents would have worked out his strengths and made plans to nullify them. His kicking skills were no longer a surprise; his kicks downfield could be combated, and a mark was no good if teams knew how to thwart the free kick. Opposing wingers could plan how to beat his defence.

In his absence Halifax lost the following match at Leeds, but then, as if to vindicate the selectors, proceeded to win 10 in a row, beginning with a 62–2 demolition of Dewsbury in which wingers Keith Williams and Johnny Freeman scored 13 tries between them, Williams claiming a club-record eight. Replacement full-back Peter Briers added another, the first of three in three matches, but stand-in goalkicker Charlie Renilson only succeeded with seven conversions. The pay deal agreed at the start of the season was £10 for a win, with an extra 10 shillings for each successive win. Luckily for the club there was a ceiling of £2 otherwise the players would have been on £15 a match by the time the winning run was ended by Wigan. Even at a steady £12 a match, Garfield was still missing out on a good income.

Frank Williams, in his analysis of the season for the *Halifax Courier*, wrote: "The fact that Garfield Owen became top scorer... makes one wonder why he was out of the side for such a long period. He was undoubtedly the most reliable goal-kicker, but many of the selectors regarded his defence as suspect. Owen, in my opinion, should have been the first choice for the full-back position. My conclusions are based on the knowledge that Owen had shown ability in defence, and confidence on the part of the selectors could easily have restored Owen's strength as a defender."

Garfield and Marlene's wedding to which Selwyn Heppenstall referred when trying to explain Garfield's axing from the team, had been six months earlier, on 23 March 1957. It was at Witley's All Saints Church in Surrey, near Marlene's home; a family wedding with no rugby representation other than some of the Halifax directors. After the reception the couple flew to Torremolinos on the Costa del Sol, where the honeymoon was spent at a villa loaned by Colonel Sewell, Marlene's uncle. Marlene was teaching at the time at Camden High School in London, where she had lived previously. While she had been to watch Garfield play when she could, she was a long way from both Newport and Halifax, and not in a position to attend often or to socialise with other players' wives.

Following the wedding, Garfield and Marlene moved to a new home at Kebroyd in Triangle near Sowerby Bridge. The welcome they received in Halifax in general, and Lower Park Royd Drive in particular, was memorable, particularly for Marlene, who had secured a teaching job at Princess Mary's Grammar School, but was not starting until September, so was home on her own during the day.

"The neighbours came round with flowers and cakes. I was quite taken aback after living in London," remembers Marlene. Mr and Mrs Wilson next door, Mr and Mrs Ballard, and Mr and Mrs Boardall became good friends. Bill Boardall was a rugby league fan, and later to become a Halifax RLFC director. He would suck on his pipe and tell them funny stories in his strong Halifax accent, which they could not fully understand and only knew to laugh when he did. Being known created problems in buying furniture for the house though, for Garfield always felt he was denied discounts because the salesmen thought he was well off. He persuaded Marlene to go instead. They were to live at Lower Park Royd Drive for more than 20 years, bringing up son Russell who was born in January 1959 and daughter Sally who came along two years later, before settling at their current home on Stafford Road.

Another local, Eric Ingham, suggested Garfield resurrect his cricketing skills by joining the local club, where Eric was vice-captain. Halifax has always had strong cricket leagues; in 1957 there was both an Amateur Association and an even better Parish League for clubs who owned their own grounds. Triangle CC, recent Parish Cup winners, played in Division 1 at Grassy Bottom, an enchanting if small venue with a rising bank of woodland on one side and tall trees and the trickling River Ryburn on the other. Garfield joined them for the 1957 season once his rugby commitments were out of the way, playing for them first against eventual champions Greetland on 25 May, alongside Eric Ingham and a notable local cricketer Dick Rodger. He played in a red cap supplied by the sponsors of his old Wales Schools international side, which seemed to provoke the Greetland batsmen to smash his bowling into the river as they rattled off Triangle's total of 111. It was suggested not very politely that he should not wear it again.

The *Halifax Courier* did not in those days print full scorecards, only noting the very best achievements in their results summary on the following Mondays. Garfield featured the next week when, at Warley, his six wickets for 13 runs helped bowl out the home side for just 74, Triangle making 78 for 4 in reply. What the newspaper failed to add was that the figures included a hat-trick.

The season was over all too quickly, with a break for the traditional Halifax Wakes Week holidays in July, matches abandoned through rain, and the Halifax rugby league season starting with the Charity Match at Huddersfield on Saturday 10 August. A problem for Garfield had been not knowing at what time the cricket matches would finish, and the consequent disruption to newly wedded home life. Added to the fact that he had taken up golf and joined Bradley Hall Golf Club, 1957 was to be his only season with Triangle. He did later play a one-off cup game for Barkisland, and appear occasionally with Halifax Nomads, a gentlemen's team whose fixture list featured Sunday matches in the Yorkshire Dales.

Back at Thrum Hall, there followed four months of 'A' team rugby after his omission on 2 November, with seemingly not a sniff of the first team. It was a situation unlikely to be repeated in the modern era, with its substitutes and long injury lists. Either Garfield or Peter Briers would just have had to play in a different position. Garfield did indeed play one game at centre for the 'A' team, but the rest of the time he was at full-back in a splendid squad that was to finish top of the league that season. Wyn Phillips, taking time to adapt to rugby league, was a regular at centre ahead of his later successful move into the pack. Garfield made 14 appearances for them, kicking 42 goals and also scoring a try.

In his absence from the first team, Halifax had exited the Challenge Cup at the second round stage, beaten 17–12 at home by Warrington in front of a crowd of 14,620. They had finished the match with just 12 players, when Peter Briers had been forced to leave the field with a fractured cheekbone. And so Garfield was recalled to the first team for the next match at Bramley on 1 March 1958, kicking six goals in a 24–10 victory. "The injury to Briers gave a glorious opportunity to Garfield Owen to live up to his price tag," recorded the *Rugby League Gazette*. "The sudden improvement in Halifax's goal-kicking record alone justified the comeback." The article added that he had remoulded his style to fit in with Halifax's current policy of placing the emphasis on attack, regularly linking with the threequarters, though this might have been more in the writer's imagination. Regardless, the rest of the season went well, and Garfield once more became a key figure in the team.

Unfortunately, it was too late for him to be able to push for inclusion in the Great Britain squad for the upcoming tour to Australia and New Zealand, the only Halifax representative being hooker Alvin Ackerley, but there was to be a consolation prize of sorts.

A few weeks later, as the team prepared to set out for a match at Featherstone, he was approached by Chairman Ted Horsfall: "I've picked you again today Garfield," he said. "And I'm also telling you that you've been selected for the Rugby League XIII." This was a representative side chosen from time to time that could include players from the whole of the league, regardless of where they were born. The team had an imminent fixture against France at Headingley on 16 April. Mr Horsfall had recently been appointed to the Council's International Committee, and the selection must have been at his recommendation, for he added, "Don't let me down!" A star-studded side included countryman Lewis Jones of Leeds, team-mate from Halifax Jack Wilkinson, and overseas crowd-pullers Brian Bevan, Tom van Vollenhoven and Keith McLellan. They all met at Headingley 90 minutes before kick-off alongside masseur H. Harrison of Hunslet, with nothing in the way of practice or preparation. While they talked to each other both in the changing rooms and on the field to arrange one or two ploys, it had to be mostly individual play.

The *Courier's* Frank Williams joined the 14,000 crowd, reporting that Garfield was an outstanding success. He "missed only one tackle throughout the game" and "his handling was of a high standard". Van Vollenhoven scored two tries and Bevan one and, after Jones had missed a few goal kicks and handed the job on, Garfield slotted over five to give his side a 19–8 victory. One of them, said Williams, was "a splendid effort from a yard inside French territory." Robert Gate in *Gone North* records how Marlene "was justifiably proud of her husband's performance, but her delight changed to outraged wrath when the radio reports of the match credited Lewis Jones with her dearest's goals."

The match was full of bright, attractive play, including speedy, entertaining handling by the French, but was marred near the end by two brawls. Alfred Drewry in the *Yorkshire Post* told how scrum-half Jeff Stevenson was seen chasing opposite number George Fages in the opposite direction to play, four colleagues from each team joining in, punching and kicking each other recklessly while the rest of the players were 50 yards away. The trainers, reserves and a touch judge pulled them apart, but it was "the longest, ugliest, most distasteful scene" he had witnessed for some time. A minute later Stevenson was battling with André Rives and another brawl ensued. Garfield's old rugby union chums might have smiled and said "We told you so," but it was no different to some of the incidents he had witnessed in his amateur days in Wales.

His winning pay was £10 (losing pay would have been £6, with £7 for a draw), plus travelling expenses. Rugby Football League secretary Bill Fallowfield was in charge, and would pay no expenses unless tickets or receipts were presented. He was fiercely protective of the kit as well, but Garfield managed to squirrel away an old England training shirt. £10 was nothing special; Halifax had increased match pay to the same £10 for the 1956–57 season, adding a further 10 shillings bonus for successive wins up to a ceiling of £2. Losing pay at Halifax was £5.

There is no call today for matches like this, but Garfield for one was grateful for it. A large attendance was attracted on a Wednesday evening, hosts Leeds benefited from 10 per cent of the gate receipts, some 3,950 programmes were sold, and the Rugby Football League made a profit of £1,524, the equivalent of around £24,000 in 2011.

During his spell in the 'A' team, Garfield had played in the first two rounds of the Yorkshire Senior Competition cup, which had brought victories over Batley 'A' and Huddersfield 'A'. This allowed him to play in the semi-final, on the Monday evening after the first team season finished, against Castleford 'A'. Halifax were awarded a penalty at one stage near the halfway line, and Garfield decided to kick for goal using a different style to gain extra length. He approached the ball from an angle in the way of modern goalkickers, and saw the ball swing in to reach its target, setting his team on the road to a 28–5 victory. In the final on 5 May Halifax faced Hull 'A' at The Boulevard, a daunting place at the best of times. He kicked a goal, and Jimmy Lawton scored a try, but they ended with only runners-up medals as Hull won 16–5. Nonetheless it was a second medal in a short space of time, sitting nicely alongside his collection of athletics and schooldays medals. The Halifax team in the final was: Owen, Mitchell, Asquith, Phillips, Renilson; Lawton, Standish, Fairbank, Taylor, Ramsden, Wynn, Marchant, Sanderson.

Garfield's two year teaching stint at Haugh Shaw ended in July. He enjoyed his time there, particularly coaching a young association football team to the final of the local schools' cup competition. He treated his team to a cinema visit on the eve of the match, with ice creams thrown in – an early attempt at what would now be called team bonding. He also bought them all tracksuits, the boys agreeing to pay him back at a shilling a week. Some of them inevitably failed to keep up with the payments, so the deal ended up costing him a fortune. It didn't work either, when they lost out in the final to Calder High School.

He had a good rapport with the kids in general, his no-nonsense, forceful manner serving him well. The kids had to walk to the Savile Park playing fields in a proper manner or it was back to school for written work. He was a stickler for clean feet in the gym. A bus driver stopped in Warley Road one time to shout across to him, "Congratulations, Mr Owen. You're the only person who can get my son to wash his feet."

He was keen to progress though. Mr Pitt, the Headmaster at Rishworth Grammar, a small independent day and boarding school with fees of £290 per annum, not too far from Garfield's Triangle home, saw the benefits of a former rugby union international on his staff to build up his school rugby teams, and offered him a job there. The recognised rugby (or "rugger") man at the school was Arthur Lomas, who Garfield recalls once explaining to all in the staff room how rugby sevens should be played, without realising Garfield's pedigree. The facilities were good, though it did seem many of the pupils were only there killing time until they could join their fathers in the family business. He taught maths and science up to 'O' Level, and also took charge of the first XV. In a school with just 234 on the roll, playing numbers were limited, the team having won just one of 12 fixtures in 1958–59.

By his second year there he had got most of them tackling in the Garfield Owen style, using their shoulders rather than their hands, and the team was successful in nine of the 12 matches played, beating the school Old Boys team for the first time in 10 years. The Junior House XV, which Garfield also coached, played five matches and won them all, scoring 122 points against 6. It was exactly what a school like Rishworth wanted, and earned him a mention in Harry Ludlam's *History of Rishworth School* written in 1973. Referring to 1961 he wrote: "Mr Garfield Owen, who had produced some excellent sports results for a period of two years, left at the end of the Lent term."

One occasion when he didn't pass to Johnny Freeman
– tackled against Warrington.

Enveloped by Wakefield loose-forward Les Chamberlain
at Belle Vue, August 1957.

Top: Garfield and Marlene.

Left: Garfield's classic goalkicking style.

# 8. Record breaker

By the time season 1958–59 began, the great Halifax side of the mid-1950s had well and truly broken up. Gone were key players Stan Kielty into retirement, John Henderson to York for £2,700, and Ken Traill to Wakefield Trinity for £1,500. None of them could be adequately replaced, though Wales was scoured again, a £2,000 offer to Swansea's recently unemployed Islwyn Hopkins being rejected. As the season progressed there were two more notable losses in hooker Alvin Ackerley and trainer-coach Dolly Dawson. Ackerley had recently returned from the 1958 Great Britain tour, but got into a row with Dawson at a training session, overheard by both spectators and directors. It was a row that had been brewing for a while, and it escalated when some players wanted a petition in support of Ackerley after he was dropped from the team by the directors.

Team spirit nosedived as others respected Dawson so much that they chose not to sign. The unwanted outcome was that both left the club, Ackerley moving to Hull KR for £750. Dawson, who had not seen eye-to-eye with the board for some time and told them a few home truths, was paid off and joined Keighley soon afterwards, bringing to an end his highly successful era at Thrum Hall. Assistant coach Stan Kielty took charge of training until Welshman Gareth Price, who had been Halifax's captain at Wembley in 1949, was appointed as Dawson's replacement.

Garfield spent most of the season as captain when he took over from his mate Geoff Palmer, who had been left out of the team on 25 October. Palmer was back the following week, but when he decided to resign the post, feeling that it was affecting his performances, Garfield was asked to continue. His new coach's view, printed by Stanley Pearson in the *Yorkshire Sports*, the *Bradford Telegraph & Argus's* weekly sports newspaper, was that "generally a captain should not be a full-back or forward; the best place for him is centre or half-back, where he is in at almost everything, but much depends on the player's personality." He thrived on the extra responsibility.

In November, Frank Williams wrote in the *Halifax Courier*: "There is no doubt the improved work of Garfield Owen has played a part in the better displays of the men now under his charge. Strangely enough, Owen has regained some of the form of the early days with the club since he was made captain of the team. The Welshman has shown the ability to lead, while Halifax now decline to use the short penalty kick inside their own half. Owen's style of play suits him and benefits the team, and he is willing to rally his players when the need arises."

John Burnett, who was himself to become a notable captain when he led the team to the League Championship title in 1965, remembers him being a good leader. "He had a great amount of respect from everybody," he says. "There were a lot of well-established players at the club who thought of rugby union men as softies, not capable of going straight into the first team. But he had done that, he was a big name, and we respected him." Other team-mates spoke of his laid-back approach. It helped with his goalkicking – he was also never ruffled if he missed a tackle – but as a leader it hindered his ability to inspire. Sport came naturally to him, so he never seemed to have to hurry. He tried to take on more responsibility. One match when the forwards were trying to batter their way out of defence, Jack Wilkinson threw the ball out to Johnny Freeman on the wing. "Jack, don't do that," shouted Garfield. "He's our match-winner." Freeman was never one to look for tacklers and would probably have been happier to let the ball roll into touch. "It gives him something to do," replied Jack. Forwards did not always appreciate the role of the outside backs, even one of the calibre of Freeman.

Tactics would often be to use the Thrum Hall slope to their advantage, trying when in possession to drag the opposition into the corner, before spinning it out to Freeman on the top side. It would involve repeated sets moving the ball up, and then back again to the bottom side, tiring the defence so they would not be able to cover. It was much slower than the modern game. Sometimes it became too intricate for the Halifax players who got lost with it, much to Garfield's consternation. "Come on," he would encourage. "Concentrate!"

The goalkicking was faring well, including his best-ever return of nine against Doncaster, and a spell of 75 successes in 19 consecutive appearances, but the run ended when he injured an ankle in the match against Bradford Northern in December. He was out for a while, feeling that he did not receive the correct treatment until after a second medical opinion was obtained. He returned to action in two 'A' team matches at the beginning of February, kicking four goals at Bramley and six at Featherstone. He was back with the seniors for the Challenge Cup first round trip to Rochdale Hornets in February, when Halifax, who had embarked on an encouraging run of form, performed unconvincingly, missed many tackles, but nevertheless won their eighth match in a row. A tricky league match at Hull Kingston Rovers was next up, but Garfield was missing again – this time for the best of reasons when more representative honours came his way.

Earlier in the season the French authorities had suggested the reintroduction of Wales into the international arena. The idea was initially turned down, but it was later agreed to send a one-off team to France. Along with John Thorley and Brian Sparks he was selected for a Welsh XIII to travel to the home of the Toulouse club, Stade des Minimes, on Sunday 1 March, though Sparks had to pull out suffering with flu. It was effectively an international match, but no caps were awarded, denying Garfield the honour of being an official dual code international. He did manage to put one over Bill Fallowfield again though, when he exchanged his Wales shirt with opposite number André Rives. The padded French number 1 shirt he now owns is a marked contrast to his lightweight rugby union equivalents.

If he had learnt French at school, instead of opting for Welsh, he might by now have been on speaking terms with Monsieur Rives, who had been the opposing French full-back in both of his League representative games. Since Rives's club side was Albi, he had also appeared in the two 1956 International Club Championship matches against Halifax, kicking two goals in Garfield's debut match, and four in the return at Thrum Hall.

Wales fielded a makeshift team in many respects, weakened by the absence of Billy Boston and Glyn Moses and without a recognised loose-forward, enough for the *Daily Express* to suggest that "at first glance Wales do not stand much chance of winning." Yet the pack in particular was still a strong one, featuring several seasoned former union stars. George Parsons in the second-row had, like Garfield, played for both Newport and Wales, hooker Tommy Harris and prop Don Vines were former Newbridge lads, while loose-forward Charlie Winslade and second-rower Dai Moses were previously with Maesteg. There was a blow when centre Lewis Jones had to cry off in midweek, for it seriously weakened the threequarter line. Travelling reserve was Bradford Northern's Halifax-born stand-off Derek Davies, nephew of Halifax's former Newport half-back Ivor; he was living at the Fountain Head Inn at Pellon and qualified through his Welsh father who was the landlord. However, the selectors also called up a specialist, Salford's one-time Cross Keys union centre John Cheshire, and it was Cheshire who won the vote for the vacant spot.

Erstwhile Huddersfield forward Bill Griffin, himself capped by Wales in 1952, contacted the Rugby Football League asking for information about the players, because he was providing commentary on Welsh radio for the BBC, who he said were also "taking a film of the game for use later". So at least there was some coverage of the team in Wales.

The team flew out from Manchester airport the day before the game, with RFL council members Frank Ridgway (Oldham) and Jim Yearsley (St Helens) in charge. Although no coach was selected — just Leigh's Bill Hughes as masseur — there was time for practice.

France fielded an equally powerful side. They proved on the day to be faster and well able to subdue the Welsh backs. The Reuter report in the *Yorkshire Post* said that it was "a disappointing match for the

25,000 spectators who watched in brilliant sunny weather. Play was rarely of the standard expected in an international, and the weakness of the Welsh back division made the match one-sided." Wales were beaten 25–8, John Cheshire and Graham Jones, once of Penarth, registering the tries and Garfield at least having the satisfaction of completing the scoring with one conversion.

Unlike with the previous season's Rugby League XIII match, there were no profits to show for the RFL — travel costs of £522, a hotel bill of 275,000 francs (£197) and players' wages of £130 not being fully covered by payments received from the French.

Following the return flight to England on the Tuesday, there was Halifax's second round cup tie to think about, the draw having presented them with the long trip to Whitehaven. The Cumbrian side had only been formed in 1948, but had beaten Halifax on every one of their four previous visits. In the absence of their three Welsh internationals, Halifax's winning run had come to an end at Hull KR, beaten fairly soundly 23–5. Peter Briers had played at full-back, as he had done in Garfield's earlier injury absence, with the goalkicking taken over by Keith Williams, now in his favoured stand-off position after his try-scoring exploits on the wing. Williams landed one but "failed with many", according to the *Courier* match report. Garfield had no reason to doubt that he would be playing at Whitehaven, but there was a shock when the team was announced after Tuesday training – he was not in it. As the team and officials assembled for departure on Friday for an overnight stay in Keswick, Garfield arrived too, with a transfer request. The inconsistency of the Thrum Hall selection committee annoyed him. They were probably hankering for a return to the recent winning run when Briers was mostly at full-back but, from his point of view, if he was good enough for an international side one week, how could he not be for Halifax the next?

Without him, the team sneaked through at Whitehaven 7–2. Loose-forward Colin Clifft became another to be dropped in its aftermath, and he, like Jack Wilkinson when it had happened to him a few weeks earlier, also demanded a transfer. Man management was clearly not a strong point among the directors.

A home draw in the third round of the cup was what everyone at the club needed now, and they got it with a plum tie against crowd-pulling Wigan. Attendances had been slipping from the previous season's average of 10,146, but the country as a whole was still in great shape and attending sports fixtures was still the thing to do on a Saturday afternoon for very many people. So if it was an important day from the players' point of view, in financial terms it was huge for the directors. The Leeds match at the same stage of the cup in 1957 had brought out the house-full notices, so they knew what to expect.

It would have to be all-ticket again, but there was a bonus in that ground improvements had included new concrete terracing at the Hanson Lane end of the ground the previous season at a cost of £8,000, paid for by the Supporters' Club. Permission was given for 30,000 tickets to be printed.

Astutely, the tickets were offered for sale at the following week's 'A' team game against Batley, drawing a much bigger crowd than the 500 who were watching the first team win at Doncaster. Garfield played in the 'A' team match, his transfer request having been refused and the matter was eventually amicably settled. Halifax 'A' won 37–14, but he was not used as goalkicker and was not recalled for the Wigan match. Nobody would have been more pleased about that than the Wigan players, officials and supporters; because when the teams had met in the league at Thrum Hall in August he had been the star man. He had scored 13 points in a stunning 25–12 Halifax triumph. "I cannot recollect any Halifax team previous to Saturday scoring 25 points in a match against Wigan," enthused Frank Williams in Monday's *Courier*.

Garfield's all round display, he said, "was one of the best from this player since he joined the club." Not only was his kicking first class, but he also opened the scoring with his first ever Halifax try. The ball had been fanned out to Johnny Freeman on the wing, Garfield supporting on the inside to take a return ball and canter the last 10 yards under the sticks.

Not being selected for the rematch in the cup meant missing out on the incentives offered by the directors, keen for more big matches. Winning pay was increased to £40 instead of the usual £10, but just £6 for a defeat or £12 for a draw. Special daylight training was organised for the Thursday before the tie, followed by an overnight stay in Ilkley on the Friday.

It all had little effect as Wigan cruised to a 26–0 victory. Bill Hughes, in his later programme notes, praised Wigan, but was not impressed by Halifax. "I dare not comment on the pathetic performance of our team," he wrote. "My disappointment at their efforts is too great." The match was not quite a sell-out, but a new club record 29,153 did buy tickets. Sales records showed that 11,300 came from Wigan, 15,000 from Halifax and the remainder from other districts, with Rochdale, Huddersfield and Keighley to the fore. The cheapest tickets were set at two shillings for adults (just £1.60 in 2011 terms) and one shilling for concessions, but receipts were still another record, £4,502.

The poor performance when it mattered against Wigan — especially failing to score — meant that Garfield was recalled for the next match. He duly continued his run of scoring in every match he played, finishing the season with 102 goals from his 28 appearances.

81

The only match he missed before the end of the season was at home to York when, in his absence through injury Halifax scored four tries but with no conversions lost 15−12.

The final match of the season was a rearranged home fixture on a Monday evening against Featherstone Rovers, which appeared of little significance. Patchy, inconsistent performances had left the team down in a disappointing 12th position, a return to where they had been in 1956−57, and the match drew only 3,985 spectators. In reality though, it mattered greatly to the directors. If Halifax won, they would finish fourth of the Yorkshire clubs, which was of great significance in determining the following season's fixtures.

In a league of 30 teams it was not possible to play everyone, the formula being to play every team in the same county, plus inter-county matches against teams of a similar standing. With 16 Yorkshire-based teams and 14 in Lancashire and Cumberland, one Yorkshire team was either nominated or volunteered to play in the Lancashire/Cumberland section. Their location near Lancashire meant that Halifax were often that team, but for the time being they were operating in Yorkshire. For the following season, the top four Yorkshire teams would have matches against Wigan, St Helens, Oldham and Swinton, plus Leeds who were the Yorkshire team in the Lancashire section. The next four Yorkshire teams would be likely to play Workington, Whitehaven, Leigh, Warrington and Widnes. From a gate-taking angle, it was vital to finish in the Yorkshire top four. "The reward for victory can be worth thousands of pounds to us," wrote Bill Hughes in his match preview programme notes. He went home happy, for Halifax won 18−12, Garfield landing three goals.

Despite the falling league gates, Halifax were managing to hold up financially. As well as the cash bonanza in the Challenge Cup, there were continued large donations from the Supporters' Club, fuelled by sales of pools tickets. The club felt able to make a huge offer of £8,000 to Oldham for star forward Derek Turner, who instead chose to sign for Wakefield Trinity, and also tried to lure former Wigan legend Jim Sullivan as coach when he finished at St Helens, only for him to opt for Rochdale Hornets, which was nearer his Wigan home. Such high-profile actions showed the ambition of the directors and would have pleased the supporters, but may have served to unsettle the existing players and coaches.

Gareth Price was indeed replaced before the 1959−60 season, by fellow Welshman Griff Jenkins, who had been at highly ranked Oldham for five years. He accepted an offer of £936 per annum plus £150 travelling expenses, way above anything paid to a coach before. Keen on sprint training, he made extensive use of a running track which had been installed behind the posts at the scoreboard end a year or two earlier, but it did nothing to improve performances. The relatively tough fixture list for a team still in the process of rebuilding resulted in a horrendous start to the season. Eight of the first nine league matches were lost, only a 21–20 success against Leeds at Headingley lightening the gloom. Defeats at Hull, Oldham, Hull KR and Bradford Northern might have been palatable, but home reversals against Featherstone Rovers, York, Swinton and the return with Oldham were not. Frank Williams in the *Courier* suggested that "the methods of Griff Jenkins and Frank Dawson are different, and for the change to be really effective it will take time," but fans unaccustomed to such failure voiced their protests, demanding this player and that be dropped.

Williams, now in the process of handing over many of his reporting duties with at the *Courier* ahead of retirement, made a feature of their views. "Some of the old faces will have to go," complained one supporter, though another inadvertently ended up complimenting Garfield when he said that "Owen ought to have double pay" after covering all the missed tackles of his colleagues. New reporter Roland Tinker took up the thread, offering his opinion that the players were not giving their best for the full 80 minutes. Of Garfield he wrote, "Owen is one whose positional sense is remarkably acute and, as he did at Odsal, is capable of linking with his attacking forces, while his kicking is invaluable," adding that "his job is made more difficult by the sackless and ineffective defensive work of the men in front of him." Garfield picked up some criticism, but avoided most of the flak. He had collected his second try for the club at Craven Park against Hull KR in September, and scored again against them at Thrum Hall a month later, in a 37–10 victory. He also kicked eight goals from 11 attempts in the Rovers match, "and with as clever a piece of handling as I have seen for some time, gave Burnett a try," wrote Tinker.

The result heralded a revival that brought 13 wins and two draws in the remaining 27 matches, but the poor start saw a lowly 22nd place finish, the worst since 1949. Yet the season saw Garfield himself at his best. "He could actually do everything," says John Burnett, "side-steps, positioning, the lot. He had a terrific brain football-wise. But his greatest strength was that he could kick goals from everywhere."

A new pair of boots had been a starting point for this 1959-60 season, but almost immediately they vanished. Under a heading "Blessing in Disguise" in his programme notes for a match in September, secretary-manager Bill Hughes told the story: "On Sunday morning last Garfield Owen was on our field practising goalkicking. After his session he took off his boots, left them on the touchline side, put on his gym shoes and joined the rest of the team for training on the cricket field. After the training he came back for his boots and found out that they were missing. On Monday night at Fartown he had to wear his old boots and strangely enough he kicked five goals out of six attempts." He added threateningly that boots were very expensive. "I hope to see them returned in due course." In fact they did reappear a couple of weeks later, brought back by a player who had inadvertently taken them thinking they were his.

Whether in new boots or not, Garfield kicked majestically throughout. He landed just one goal from four attempts when Halifax were beaten 17–5 by the Australian tourists in front of 8,294 spectators on 7 November, but by the last match of the season he was on 146 goals, needing four more at Castleford to overhaul the Halifax club record of 149, set by his predecessor, Tuss Griffiths, in 1955–56.

Halifax lost the match 20–14, but Garfield got his four goals. There were three in the first half to equal the record then, in the second, he kicked an amazing drop-goal, worth two points at the time, which he always regarded as one of his finest kicks. Frank Williams, still writing occasionally in the *Courier*, described it as "one of the most brilliant dropped goals I have ever seen", from three yards inside the Castleford half, "and not above three yards from the touchline, a kick worthy of breaking any record."

There was, though, to be a sting in the tail. Some 20 years later a Rugby Football League directive ruled that goals kicked in friendly matches should not count, and Garfield had landed five in the pre-season charity match at Huddersfield. Modern day friendly matches, with their sheer frequency and myriad substitutions, are indeed unworthy of inclusion, but the annual encounter with Huddersfield, originally for the Infirmary Cup, was a completely different matter. Garfield's seasonal total was adjusted to 145 and Griffiths's to 147, enough to retain the record above him. It has in any case since been superseded by the 156 potted by Graham Holroyd in 2008.

To kick even 145 goals was a remarkable achievement. The team as a whole scored only 133 tries, Garfield's own two helping give him a points total of 296, one short of Griffiths's record 297. He played in all 44 matches, including Christmas Day and Boxing Day against Huddersfield and, on April 16, 18 and 19 over Easter. His value to the team had also increased markedly in January, when the Rugby League Council abolished the tap penalty, forcing teams to kick to touch; no-one could do that better than him. "It seems that Halifax full-back Garfield Owen has been quickest to adapt himself to the kicking technique which the Rugby League's mid-season rule change demands," commented Lewis Jones in a national newspaper column. "Hardly surprising, however, for Owen was the last full-back out of the classic mould of Welsh kickers to turn pro'."

An important part of successful kicking was the ball itself. This may no longer be the case with modern developments having standardised the shape, size, weight and appearance, but in the years that Garfield played this was not the case. It was annoying to him that his own club paid little regard to such vital equipment. These were the days before sponsorship deals for kit and rugby balls, and they were items to be neglected when economies needed to be made. Halifax had a particularly misshapen, lopsided ball with uneven slanted panels, and he urged Bill Barrett, the kit man whose domain this was, to get rid of it, but Bill never took heed. Garfield tried booting it over the stands and out of the ground whenever the opportunity arose, but it was always brought back; without it there probably would not have been enough to get by. Incidentally, Bill Barrett, who was involved at Thrum Hall for many years, had a fine collection of player action photographs. The *Halifax Courier* printed off heaps of such photographs and would leave them on the table in the changing rooms at training sessions for players to help themselves to those on which they appeared. Bill always acquired a few, which he put into enormous albums.

With Garfield's success, Peter Briers battled on in the reserves, but even that place came under threat in November when Halifax recruited another young Welsh full-back from Garfield's old club Maesteg — Ronnie James. Ronnie, considered close to a Welsh rugby union cap, had long been a supporter of his national team, travelling in the mid-1950s with his local pub to the terraces at Cardiff Arms Park to watch his hero, none other than Garfield Owen. "He was an idol of mine; I can honestly say that," acknowledged Ronnie in later years. Now he was joining the same team. Peter Briers moved on to Castleford to contest the full-back position at his home-town club.

Live televising of rugby league matches on the BBC's Saturday afternoon *Grandstand* programme had started the previous season, and Halifax's home first round Yorkshire Cup tie against Wakefield Trinity on 29 August became the first match from Thrum Hall to be featured. Wakefield, challenging for the league leadership all season, were to be Wembley winners in May, so were probably the attraction to the BBC rather than Halifax. The belief in rugby league at the time was that showing matches live on television was reducing crowds, but the attendance at this match was a healthy 12,508. Remarkably Halifax won 17–14, Garfield kicking four goals, with tries coming from veteran stand-off Ken Dean with two and winger Alan Snowden.

Ever eager to enliven his commentaries, the BBC commentator Eddie Waring told viewers that the "garryowen" to which Garfield refers in his introduction and was a common rugby union term for the up-and-under or bomb, was named after Halifax's Garry Owen.

Although entirely plausible, it was far from the truth, which was that the term originated from the Garryowen rugby union club in

Breaking through between Lewis Jones (right) and
Garry Hemingway against Leeds in August 1958.

Garfield and Bryn Jones arrive too late to prevent a try for Oldham's
Charlie Winslade at Thrum Hall, September 1958.

Wales Rugby League XIII, 1959. Back: John Thorley, Don Vines, Malcolm Davies, Rees Thomas, John Cheshire, Charlie Winslade, Gordon Lewis, George Parsons, Dai Moses; front: Garfield Owen, Tommy Harris, Lionel Emmett, Graham Jones.

Halifax 1959-60. Back: Brian Sparks, Charlie Renilson, Trevor King, Frank Fox, Fred Turnbull, Colin Clifft, Johnny Freeman; front: Garfield Owen, Alan Snowden, Ken Dean, Bryn Jones, John Burnett, Geoff Palmer.

Limerick, Ireland who, between 1924 and 1926, had won three senior cups using that tactic to the utmost. Garfield later sought out Eddie to correct him, but to no avail; he continued to repeat what he thought was a good story.

After the match Wakefield signed Halifax's Jack Wilkinson, a blow to the spectators, if not some of the directors who felt he was past his best. Jack had not trained since the previous season and had been transfer-listed at £7,500, but Wakefield negotiated the fee down to £4,500. Jack became a key player in Wakefield's glory years of the early 1960s. At the same time Halifax made their own serious efforts to rebuild their team. A £6,000 bid for Hunslet's Great Britain forward Brian Shaw was turned down, but a club record £7,500 was splashed out to bring local forward Jack Scroby home from Bradford Northern. Although Jack himself had a distinguished career with the club, the team-building efforts were for the time being unsuccessful, the directors in the club minutes lamenting a lack of experience, so unlike the glory years.

Garfield's scoring run continued into season 1960−61, when he played in 41 of the 42 matches and added another 130 goals. The home match against St Helens on 18 March was his 81st consecutive appearance, a run ended when he made way for Ronnie James to debut at Batley the following week. Only Dick Davies, a full-back from the 1920s, had played in more consecutive games, 106, for Halifax.

Garfield landed three goals when Halifax played a match against the New Zealand international side, who were in England for the 1960 World Cup tournament, staged between 24 September and 8 October. All three visiting World Cup teams, France, New Zealand and Australia, had agreed to play one extra fixture, and Halifax were granted the Kiwi game. Unfortunately it had an inconvenient kick-off time, 4.00pm on the afternoon of Wednesday 12 October, and a crowd of just 1,960 saw Halifax beaten 18−12.

The World Cup itself was won by Great Britain, who also mastered a Rest of the World selection two days after it ended. Garfield, without a strong team to play behind, had found himself out of contention for a place in the squad.

Halifax had volunteered to be the Yorkshire team to play in the Lancashire/Cumberland section, no doubt stimulated by a Rugby Football League subsidy of £1,000. Their lowly finish the previous year meant that their Yorkshire opponents were Bramley, Batley, Keighley and Huddersfield, rather than teams like Leeds, Wakefield and Hull. There were the inevitable repercussions of lower attendances, but in compensation the lower opposition allowed them to get on something of a roll and by December they actually headed the league table. They fell away disappointingly thereafter, winning only six more games to finish 13th, but it was a step in the right direction. Garfield kicked his 100th goal of the season, and his 500th in total for Halifax, at the Recreation Ground, Whitehaven, on Good Friday, and three days later scored his fourth Halifax try, against Barrow at Thrum Hall, a match in which he rattled up 17 points.

A distraction to the league form had been a successful run in the Challenge Cup. Mid-table Hunslet had been beaten at Parkside in the first round, and higher-placed Workington Town at Derwent Park in the second. An anonymous match report of the Workington tie in the *Daily Express* said that the Town players had been given strict instructions to avoid infringements which would give goalkicking opportunities, but they did so in the first minute and again in the second half, Garfield making them pay both times to give Halifax a 4–0 victory. "They were remarkable kicks in the heavy conditions from only three yards short of the half-way line." Workington enjoyed a 12–3 advantage in the first half penalty count, but "neither Ike Southward nor Sid Lowden could match the accuracy of Owen." Lowden was his old colleague from the Oswestry army days. Johnny Freeman has vivid memories of the encounter. "The ball was like a piece of soap and Workington kept putting up high kicks to my wing. Garfield was always there to help. 'Yours!' I shouted clearly every time, and he never dropped one. He was as safe as houses under a kick."

After twice bowing out at the third round stage since their last appearance in the final, a home draw against Rochdale Hornets, third from the bottom of the table with only Liverpool City and Doncaster below them, was welcome. For the directors it would be less of a financial bonanza than a top team would have brought, but they dipped into the coffers to put the big money on offer to the players again. There was no need this time for the tie to be all-ticket, yet sales of stand seats were buoyant, the attendance still reaching 17,167, easily a season-high, producing receipts of £2,191. The first half of the game was filmed by the BBC, for highlights to be shown on their *Sport in the North* programme. They stayed long enough to record Garfield kicking three penalty goals, tries from John Burnett and Johnny Freeman, and Rochdale points from a Simms try and Atherton goal, to give a half-time score of 12–5. Later Geoff Palmer and Johnny Freeman crossed the whitewash, and Frank Fox was sent off after an incident with Parr 14 minutes from the end to leave Halifax short-handed, but they won easily enough, 18–5. Welshman Wyn Phillips was picked out by the *Halifax Courier* as the star man in a strong Halifax performance but, wrote Roland Tinker, "Behind them all was the safe and sound Garfield Owen, a man whose football week after week should have made him an automatic choice for Great Britain." He then added that his goalkicking was not up to standard, his three successes coming from 11 attempts. As far as the statisticians were concerned that left him on 99 for the season, five second-half attempts to reach the century all going wide. Their figures included three in the Huddersfield charity match though, later discounted. What no one was aware of because of these later qualification changes was that in the match Garfield reached 1,000 career points for Halifax, only the second player after Hubert Lockwood to do so.

An appearance in the final at Wembley was every player's dream, there now being only two, Johnny Freeman and Geoff Palmer, who remained from the 1956 final. A younger generation including Barry Robinson, Charlie Renilson, Frank Fox and Jack Scroby had stepped up to the mark. For Garfield, Wembley would have sat nicely alongside Twickenham and Cardiff Arms Park. The semi-final draw paired Halifax with Wigan at Station Road, Swinton, the directors once more offering the incentive of £40 per man for victory. The Thrum Hallers would need to be at their absolute peak; Wigan were huge favourites, especially after beating Halifax at Central Park in a league match the previous week.

Garfield kicked two goals, Johnny Freeman and Jack Scroby scored tries, but it was not to be, the bookies being proved right when Wigan triumphed 19–10. "Instead of being well above form, I thought we played just a little below our best," was Bill Hughes's opinion expressed in the following match programme. "At one stage I thought Wigan might have run away with us, but for twenty five minutes in the second half we played our best football and came within an ace of the Wigan lead." There was an attendance of 35,398, which might have unnerved some of the Halifax youngsters, but to Garfield, just as in his union days, it never bothered him.

"It didn't matter how many people were there," he says. "It never entered my head that I might miss a kick – until I did!" *Daily Express* writer Harvey Stead reported that "full-backs Garfield Owen and Fred Griffiths just about matched each other (one catch of Owen's of a ball swinging into touch was little short of miraculous) but nowhere else — man for man — did Halifax come anywhere near the Wigan standard." If the third round defeats in 1957 and 1959 were big disappointments, this one was massive.

For Garfield personally it had been a good season, and it ended with an honour. The Halifax Supporters' Club, formed way back in 1923 as a fund-raising body and vehicle for fans to share their love of the team, followed a trend set by others and established a Player-of-the-Season competition in 1960–61, casting votes after every match. Wingers Johnny Freeman and Alan Snowden, centres Geoff Palmer and John Burnett, and forwards Jack Scroby and captain Brian Sparks were in contention, but the winner was Garfield. The award is still made every season, but the original trophy is lost, believed to be in Australia with one of its 1980s winners.

It was not his only award. The various supporters' groups in Yorkshire were affiliated to the Yorkshire Federation of Supporters' Clubs, who presented an annual Jim Harrison Trophy to the fairest and most loyal player in the county. Jim Harrison had been a Bramley Supporters' Club official who had died while in office as chairman of the federation, the trophy having been donated by his widow in 1958. Chosen by a panel of Lancashire referees, earlier winners had been Wakefield Trinity's Eric Cooper, Doncaster's Fred Williamson, and Huddersfield's Ted Slevin. No player epitomised fairness more than Garfield, the ultimate sportsman who had hardly ever even been penalised in an era when players were quite regularly sent off.

He can remember just one blemish, in a match at The Boulevard, Hull, when he made a complete hash of a high ball and promptly hoofed it 50 yards downfield; the referee ordered him to go and fetch it. Luckily that referee was not on the selection panel, and since he qualified for the loyalty part of the requirements by having stayed with Halifax for nearly five years, he was adjudged the winner.

With the Player-of-the-Season title, almost a Wembley appearance, and another haul of more than 100 goals in a season under his belt, Garfield would seem to have been set for a long stay at Halifax, but in fact he played only two more matches.

Halifax team 1960–61. Back: Fred Turnbull, Wyn Phillips, Frank Fox, Charlie Renilson, Johnny Freeman, Alan Snowden, Jack Scroby, John Burnett; front: Barry Robinson, Alan Marchant, Trevor Taylor, Garfield Owen, Geoff Palmer.

Garfield was the inaugural winner of the Halifax Supporters' Club Player of the Season award in 1961. The trophy was presented by president Fred Stringer.

# 9. Moving on

Ronnie James had been starring for the second team, so was given a run in the pre-season charity match at Huddersfield in early August 1961. Huddersfield were to finish fourth in the league, but impressive Halifax beat them 18–13. So it was a disappointment and frustration to all when, with Garfield back in the side, the first official fixture at Oldham was lost, followed by a 10–10 draw at Thrum Hall against Bramley. It was an important season, for at the end of it the league was to be split into two divisions. There would be no chicanery from the Rugby Football League, or modern-day franchises – the top 16 clubs in the final table would comprise Division 1 in 1962–63.

Garfield's pal Geoff Palmer had opted to retire from the game for business reasons at the tender age of 26, bringing to an end the formidable centre partnership that had been developing with John Burnett, but Colin Dixon was there to replace him, and the team should have been performing better. The directors perceived a lack of determination and attacking skill. They had by now moved forwards by encompassing the views of trainer-coach Griff Jenkins on team selection. He attended the weekly board meetings to make recommendations on which players should be chosen for the first and second teams for all matches. The recommendations were subject to confirmation by the directors, who retained the last say, but they claimed that they gave every consideration and support to his views.

The Football Sub-committee in any case now included a couple of former players, existing members Heppenstall and Rushworth being joined by Cyril Stacey, a Great Britain tourist from the 1920s and recent 'A' team coach, and Welsh international Dai Rees, who had led Halifax at Wembley in 1931 and had extensive coaching and managing experience with Bradford Northern. Between them, they opted to bring in Ronnie James, a very different kind of full-back to Garfield, not as technically efficient, but noted for his surging runs out of defence and keenness to join the attack. The new full-back did not transform the team, but he did hold his place and help Halifax scrape into Division 1 by finishing 15th.

The drawn game against Bramley back on 21 August proved to be Garfield's last match for the first team, though there was to be a swansong in mid-September. New Zealand were over for a tour, the Rugby Football League coming up with the idea of pairing them against combined teams. Having played against such as Swinton/Salford, Castleford/Featherstone, Leeds/Bramley/Hunslet and Oldham/Rochdale, they met Huddersfield/Halifax on Saturday 16 September. Six Halifax players — Colin Dixon, Johnny Freeman, Alan

Marchant, John Shaw, Roger Crabtree and Garfield — travelled over to Huddersfield's Fartown ground to join the team. A crowd of 7,251 saw the tourists win 31–11, Garfield kicking one goal for the combined Huddersfield and Halifax team.

Other than that, it was another, unexpected, spell of second team football. In October Griff Jenkins was offered a coaching role at Wigan, a prize job nearer his Leigh home, and Halifax agreed to release him. His assistant Albert Fearnley, who as a player had left Halifax a month before Garfield arrived, was promoted into his place, aided by his former team-mate Stan Kielty, another who was already on the staff. There was no accompanying change in selection policy though. Garfield continued in the 'A' team, where he kicked 44 goals in nine appearances. The last was a home game on 25 November against Bradford Northern, which was where it had all begun five years ago. He signed off with 12 goals in a 54–0 rout.

By then he had made up his mind that he would have to leave. Ronnie James was a younger man who was playing well. "Ronnie proved to be what the Halifax public wanted," recalls Garfield, "a graceful finisher of attacking ploys." First team opportunities for Garfield would clearly be limited. 'A' team pay was quite low, £4 for a win and £2 10/- (£2 50p) for a defeat, compared with £11 and £6 in the seniors, so he asked to be placed on the transfer list. In due course Keighley showed interest. The news was released to the public in the programme for the Batley match on 13 January: "It is confirmed that Keighley have been given permission to approach Garfield Owen. The outcome of the negotiations between Keighley and the player are not known as this programme is being written. Should Garfield decide to join Keighley then we shall be sorry to see him leave Thrum Hall. But he is much too good a player to be languishing in 'A' team football. He merits a first team place. We are fortunate (or maybe unfortunate) to have two full-backs of the calibre of Garfield Owen and Ronnie James. One has to play in the 'A' team and for most of this season it has been Garfield's lot to be the reserve. It is understandable therefore if he does decide to go for a first team place in Keighley's team. The onus of the move will be entirely upon the player."

The decision was an easy one for him. Keighley had recently bought their ground from the Duke of Devonshire's estate and were a friendly, well-run club, playing at a scenic location with a steep, picturesque hillside as a backdrop, just a dozen or so miles away from his home. They were in a similar league position to Halifax, even if in the last five seasons they had finished 20th, 22nd, 15th, 20th and 25th in the final tables, watched by crowds hovering around the 3,000 level. In the pre-Super League era all teams were more evenly matched, with most of them quite capable of beating any other on their day.

Garfield had certainly never found Keighley an easy team to play against, having lost to them on four of the seven occasions he had opposed them with Halifax. Their winger Terry Hollindrake had played for Great Britain in 1955 ahead of a recent £6,000 transfer to Hull, and they had some decent players. One who particularly stood out was stand-off Roy Sabine, who Garfield remembered skipping past him for a hat-trick at Thrum Hall some years earlier.

The Keighley chairman, John Smallwood, came across well and made him feel wanted. Mr Smallwood was an estate agent and auctioneer who had built up the agency of Dacre, Son and Hartley into a large concern in the area and had led Keighley's board since 1953. He pointed out that four or five matches that season had been lost by only a few points, with goalkicking misses having been crucial; Garfield was just what they needed at Lawkholme Lane. It was the sort of comment he wanted to hear and his mind was made up. "I don't think I have anything to lose by moving to Keighley," he told the *Daily Express*'s Jack Bentley. "I reckon I've another two years before I retire from playing." The deal was signed, and he met a host of new, good people, none more so than secretary Bill Spencer and baggage man Billy Watson, who both looked after him royally. Spencer served as secretary for 27 years, while Watson was a former Keighley international hooker of the 1930s who, after moving to Huddersfield, had become the first and possibly only Keighley-born player to appear in a Challenge Cup Final at Wembley, in 1935.

Match pay varied little between clubs in the 1960s, so as long as Keighley won sufficient matches the move would work out well financially. Keen to add to his travelling expenses though, he asked how other Halifax-based players, such as former Siddal, Bradford Northern and York centre Brian Todd, travelled to Keighley, and was told the club hired taxis for them. Very few players owned cars at this time, but Garfield did. He asked that the taxi firm be notified they were no longer required, and became the taxi himself, working out a route from Halifax through Queensbury, Denholme and Oxenhope to pick up others on the way and earn a tidy sum. He owned a secondhand Hillman Minx in 1961, but was soon to move into the motor trade, which allowed him to use a larger company pool car and accommodate his passengers more comfortably.

Rugby League byelaw 19 stated that "a player on the transfer list at his own request shall receive no percentage of the transfer fee"; those listed at the club's request and with at least five years' service were entitled to five per cent. Garfield, however, had negotiated in his original contract with Halifax that he would receive 10 percent of any future transfer fee from both Halifax and his new club. The transfer fee agreed with Keighley was £3,200, a new record for the Lawkholme

Laners, so he received £320 from both clubs. It was a significant sum, as in 1962 a new car, such as a Ford Cortina, cost £591.

There was disappointment in Halifax that he had left. The *Courier's* Roland Tinker felt no-one could blame him for leaving, but that the Halifax directors should have retained him. "What happens if Ronnie James is injured?" he asked. "For the last five months Owen, one of the few natural footballers at Thrum Hall, has been wasted in the second team. He is a brilliant and thoughtful player, who, during the past few years, has been on the shortlist for Great Britain. When a club has got two players of such talent as Owen and James for the same position, they should utilise them both by playing one out of position. That might not be possible if the Halifax back section was moving with such devastation as Wigan's or Wakefield Trinity's, but it is not, and there have been ample opportunities to experiment."

There were letters to the *Courier* supporting Tinker's view and urging that the transfer be aborted. 'Unashamedly Biased' wrote that "there is room, and need, for the talents of both Owen and James in the team, and I have no doubt that such a solution would give satisfaction to supporters and add greatly to the team's effectiveness." Another, 'The Black Cat' suggested that Garfield should be at full-back, with Ronnie James on the wing, and J. Thompson of Highfield Place observed that Garfield "without a doubt is the finest full-back Thrum Hall has had since Lockwood" and proposed James for a half-back role. In the 21st century, Ronnie James, with his lightning play-the-balls in an era when such were virtually unknown, and his powerful running, could have made a hooker in the Keiron Cunningham mould. It was all immaterial. Both wanted to play full-back and for Garfield that meant a change of club.

He was by this time no longer in teaching. Without a degree to his name, he felt his opportunities in that profession were limited, and that the potential for greater financial reward lay elsewhere. He quit his post at Rishworth, and answered an advertisement in the *Yorkshire Post* for a salesman for Canada Life insurance. It went well for a time, but through golf at Bradley Hall he met Colin Swain, a local businessman who ran Hoffman's Garage. Hoffman's sold cars at the top end of the range, Rolls Royce and Bentley. "Tell me how much you want," he was told, "and we'll see what you can do." It was the start of a long association with the motor industry.

Coach and captain at Keighley in 1961 was stand-off-half Gordon Brown, a fleeting acquaintance from National Service days. An illustrious career had seen him play more than 250 matches for Leeds and six for Great Britain, including the first World Cup Final in 1954, before he had joined Keighley in 1960. He had been turning out occasionally at full-back himself and taking a few of the goalkicks in the absence of a specialist in both, so was pleased to welcome Garfield into the team. Both the local press and the match programme often took to referring to Garfield as Garry Owen, maybe having listened too much to Eddie Waring.

Icy conditions meant that Keighley had not played for a month when he finally put pen to paper on the Friday evening of 12 January 1962, but the home match with Castleford went ahead at Lawkholme Lane the following afternoon. Brown moved to centre to accommodate Garfield at full-back in the following team: Owen, M. Smith, Brown, Todd, G. Jackson, Edwards, Hebden, R. Bloomfield, Anderson, Fall, Phillips, Haigh, V. Jackson.

Higher-placed Castleford, with Alan Hardisty in their team but not his injured half-back partner Keith Hepworth, were tough opponents and there was to be no dream debut. "The introduction of overnight signing from Halifax Garfield Owen did not have the effect of inspiring the home side," wrote the correspondent in the local weekly newspaper *The Keighley News*, "despite him kicking three first half goals which gave Keighley a one-point lead at the change round." Backed by a strong wind, he was able to put in some hefty touch-finding kicks, but in the second period the forwards were badly beaten for possession and, despite one noteworthy try-saving tackle, Keighley faded to lose 16–6.

"Have Halifax made their biggest post-war blunder?" asked Stanley Pearson of *Yorkshire Sports*. "Judging by James's display at Thrum Hall on Saturday, compared with colleague Eric Lund's impression of Owen at Lawkholme, they have erred badly. James kicked two goals from eleven attempts, while his touch-finding and runs were so rare they were hardly noticeable. At Keighley, Owen, playing with new colleagues and on a strange ground, landed three goals from five." Lund had reported that Garfield had played exceptionally well, his touch-finding and defence had been remarkable, and he "was the best Keighley player".

However, Keighley's hopes of Division One qualification ebbed as further defeats followed in the next couple of weeks at Hunslet and Wakefield Trinity, before the next home game against Doncaster brought Garfield's first win in his new emerald-green and scarlet colours. He had an off-day with his kicking, landing only one from five attempts, but it was an important victory ahead of the first round of the Challenge Cup, in which Keighley had been given home advantage against league leaders Wigan. In a throwback to the big ties at Thrum Hall, the club organised special daylight training on the Thursday afternoon, followed by a get-together meal in the town. Advance ticket sales passed the £1,000 mark, a healthy crowd of 9,700 eventually turning up. Their hopes took a knock when Geoff Crewdson had to withdraw, Wigan duly proving to be too strong and easing into a 15–3 lead by half-time. Gordon Brown crossed wide out, but in the second half had to leave the field with a dislocated shoulder, as Wigan ended 25–3 winners. "Keighley did their best," reported the local press, "but unfortunately it was nowhere near good enough."

An even bigger occasion for Garfield was the following week's return to Thrum Hall to face Halifax. Gordon Brown was out, adding even more spice to the highly anticipated Owen versus James clash when Garfield was chosen to replace him as captain. But there was to be more disappointment for him when, for a second major game in succession, he was unable to score, and Ronnie James collected a try and four goals, in Keighley's 20–3 defeat.

There were a few wins in the weeks to come, including revenge over Halifax on 10 April when he kicked five goals in a 25–10 success. Record try-scorer Johnny Freeman, a long-time admirer of his defensive qualities, came up against him for the first time, having been absent at Thrum Hall. "He was a brilliant tackler," he comments. "If you ran straight at him, you could beat him, but if he forced you to run at an angle he could time it brilliantly and catch you. He cut across, and no matter how fast you were, he got you."

There was also a thrilling victory against York at Clarence Street, his penalty 15 minutes from the end edging Keighley 9–7 ahead, a lead they were able to hold. Remembering John Smallwood's tales of close matches being lost for want of a reliable goal-kicker, it was a significant moment that built his confidence. At Hull Kingston Rovers a week later the *Keighley News* reported that "Owen in particular was superb." Try saving tackles kept his team in the game, but, as a last line of defence, physical danger always lurked. He "took a terrific hammering as he fielded from the feet of the Hull forwards. He had the ball taken from his grasp and the Rovers wingman was over." Keighley were beaten 14–5 on their way to a 19th place finish. It was one place above where they had been when Garfield signed, but nine league points adrift of Hull, who took the 16th place to join the prospective First Division.

He had played in all the 18 first team matches since signing for the club, in which he had kicked a total of 44 goals. "Owen has pleased everybody and his goalkicking ability has stood Keighley in good stead," summarised the local press, observing that he had filled a long-felt want, the full-back berth having been a headache since the retirement of Joe Phillips. The scoring rate was helped by a farmer friend of one of the Keighley directors who travelled on the team coach. He offered Garfield 10 shillings for each try he scored – his money was fairly safe there – and more significantly two shillings for every goal. Garfield tried for goal whenever he could.

The move to two divisions was a controversial one. It had been tried before in the early part of the century, but soon abandoned when the Second Division clubs found it hard to survive with poor crowds. In the 1960s, the top clubs wanted it again, just like they do in the present day with Super League. Regular matches against other top clubs would boost their crowds and takings. They had little understanding, or maybe even care, for clubs left out of the top flight, persuading them that competitive matches against clubs of the same standard would be a benefit, and that meaningless matches would be removed with promotion and relegation to fight for or against. The plan, formulated a year earlier in response to declining crowds after the 1950s boom, was to run it as an experiment for three seasons, after which another vote would be necessary for it to continue. A majority of clubs had voted in favour, with only eight against. League chairman Ted Horsfall, from Halifax, told clubs that "it has been a long time coming, but it will bring about beneficial results that will stagger some people. I am sure this will result in bigger attendances."

One delegate from a lower club had said that gates were now so low anyway that there was nothing to lose. It wasn't Keighley's John Smallwood, who was strongly opposed, but it certainly could have been, since only Dewsbury, Blackpool Borough, Bradford Northern, Doncaster and Liverpool City had a lower aggregate in 1961–62 than Keighley. Figures produced by Ramon Joyce[*] for the *Rugby Leaguer* newspaper showed a total attendance of 37,950 for 18 home matches, an average of 2,108.

In this spirit Keighley, like others, started the new Second Division 1962–63 season with confidence. The *Keighley News* noted there was an "obvious chance of achieving promotion at the first attempt." Some supporters were concerned at the lack of new signings, one fan at the Annual General Meeting threatening to go and watch John Charles at Leeds United instead. Ken Pye was recruited from Castleford to strengthen the forwards, but cash for new players was limited. The club had made a loss of £977 on 1961–62, with gate receipts totalling £4,326 when players' wages alone were £5,509. Like at Halifax it was donations from the Supporters' Club, £10,461 on this occasion, which kept the club going.

Before the league season though, there was a series of games to negotiate in a new Eastern Region Competition, designed to maintain local derbies, many of which had been lost in the new set-up. Each team opposed four others in home and away fixtures, the results being fed into a table for the whole county. A similar Western Region competition took place in Lancashire. Keighley's matches were against

---

* The pseudonym for Raymond Fletcher, the *Yorkshire Post* journalist

99

Bramley, Castleford, Hull KR and Halifax, a difficult proposition in that the corresponding league fixtures the previous season had brought just five points, from wins over Bramley and Halifax at home and a draw at Bramley. So it was no great surprise when only two of the games were won, at home to Bramley and Castleford, and they failed to qualify for the top-4 play-offs. Gordon Brown played in the match at Halifax in August, but that turned out to be his last appearance. Perhaps fearing that this might happen, the club had already appointed Garfield as captain for the season.

Brown, who remained as coach, got his team fit and enthusiastic for the more important league campaign, victories coming on a regular basis against the easier opposition. There was a boost when former player Derek Hallas, who had been at Leeds, returned for a 14-match spell ahead of his planned move to Australia. By Christmas they had won all except one game, at Barrow, when Hallas was sent off, and topped the table. Major challengers Hunslet had defied the odds to win the Yorkshire Cup, beating First Division Wakefield Trinity, Hull, Halifax in the semi-final, then Hull KR, but had lost at Liverpool City the week before the final. Keighley then beat Hunslet 21–4 on 1 December at Lawkholme Lane, Garfield kicking six goals.

It was a major inconvenience when mid-winter brought 1963's long-lasting big freeze. There were no matches for Keighley between 22 December and 2 March, and none at home from 15 December until 23 March, almost as long as the previous close-season. Regular trips to training across the snow-bound moors from Halifax became a bind for Garfield with a Saturday match not even remotely likely, although every other team was in the same boat.

When play was able to recommence, Keighley travelled to Hull KR for a delayed Challenge Cup tie, 10,000 watching the home side scrape through 6–5 in thick, icy-cold, clinging mud. The *Keighley News* described the ground as "like the bottom of the docks at low tide." Garfield had a chance to win the game just before the final hooter with a penalty attempt from 40 yards out, but "a brave attempt dipped just under the bar."

Promotion rivals Hunslet meanwhile won their match at Rochdale, then beat Halifax again at Thrum Hall, before losing narrowly 7–5 at Warrington in the third round. Keighley were able to focus on their league programme, but were unable to press home the advantage when they were narrowly beaten at York and Doncaster. As the extended season neared its conclusion, Keighley and Hunslet had still surged away from the others in the quest for both the championship and the two promotion places. The two met at Parkside on 27 April for what was looking like a title decider, a crowd of 7,600 reflecting its importance.

Keighley team 17 February 1962. Back: Harold Fall, Billy Sharpe, Brian Wright, Syd Phillips, Syd Hebden, Eric Redman, Mel Smith; front: Alan Edwards, Geoff Dudley, Roy Bleasby, Garfield Owen, Brian Todd, Dick Bloomfield.

Autographs for admiring young fans at Keighley, after the last home match of the promotion winning 1962−63 season.

Hunslet took initial control of a thrilling game, but Keighley fought back to trail by just 10–9 as the final whistle neared, Garfield having converted Albert Eyre's try and kicked two penalty goals. As so often happened there were chances to win; either of two further penalty chances in the closing minutes would have brought victory, but both long-range shots fell short and Hunslet held on. "After a hard battle it was natural that even Owen could not find the strength which had produced the fine goals in the early part of the game," reported the *Keighley News*.

Hunslet were now frontrunners for the championship, but when they slipped up at Leigh the following week, all was not lost. Three successive victories sent Keighley back to the top by a points average difference of 0.056 with just four matches left to play, three of them at home where they were unbeaten in the league and on a run of 11 consecutive wins. The first was against mid-table Rochdale Hornets, but what seemed like a formality provided a final cruel twist when Keighley suffered a shock 14–13 reversal in high wind and driving rain. Garfield converted a Mel Smith try and added a penalty, "both magnificent kicks from near touch", but in the second half, "apart from Owen's three penalty goals, they never looked like scoring". Garfield was up in the attack, having had to change positions with injured stand-off Roy Sabine, and in desperation attempted a drop-goal with three minutes remaining, but the ball hardly rose from the ground. The final minute brought the seemingly obligatory penalty chance, from 45 yards out – a last chance to save the day – but he was not to be a hero this time. "Owen failed to rise to the occasion," commented the local newspaper.

By the time of their last match of the season on 29 May, a Wednesday night, Keighley travelled to bottom-of-the-table Bradford Northern still adrift by the two points dropped against Rochdale. A large win was needed to put pressure on Hunslet, who faced a tricky journey to fourth-placed Blackpool Borough the following night. Garfield had his holidays booked, the season having been scheduled to finish some weeks earlier, but took the decision to turn out. "To enable him to play at Odsal," reported the *Keighley News*, "Owen is delaying his holiday and will travel by special flight the following day." It was the family's first holiday abroad, for normally they had stayed with parents in either Wales or Surrey, but Marlene's father had a flat in Spain that they had arranged to use. While Marlene and the kids sunned themselves in Fuengirola, then a small fishing village, Garfield was in Bradford.

He kicked five goals, Roy Sabine scored a hat-trick, and Keighley won 25–6. Points average was so much more complicated than the modern system of points difference, but the title could be Keighley's if

Hunslet lost. Their match was close, Blackpool outscored them two tries to one, but Hunslet prevailed 13–10 to clinch the championship. Keighley were runners-up. They had won 21 of their 26 league matches to secure the second promotion position, nine points clear of third-placed York. If the end was anti-climactic, it was still a notable achievement. Congratulatory telegrams had not yet completely died out, one arriving at Lawkholme Lane from Keighlians Rugby Union club, a reciprocal compliment to that paid to them when they had beaten Otley to win the 1948 Yorkshire Cup Final.

Some Second Division teams might have been struggling, but Keighley's success had brought significantly improved attendance figures, the average rising to 2,706. It was still not enough to cover the wages, but other income streams also increased. Malcolm Davies, the former Leigh and Bradford Northern player who had been a team-mate of Garfield's in the 1959 Welsh side, joined the staff to organise the daily draw run by the Supporters' Club, a position he had previously filled at Bradford. The draw had been showing a profit of £350 a week, but there were hopes for even more. Further income for the club came from a petrol filling station on their land beside the ground entrance, leased to Grace and Sutcliffe. Major alterations were due in that area with the Keighley by-pass scheduled for later in the year, necessitating the setting back of the boundary wall on Hard Ings Road.

Garfield had a tremendous year, winning plaudits in end-of-season press summaries. Ken Pye was acclaimed as the pick of the forwards, but "in the backs Garry Owen must take the honours for his consistently good goalkicking and also for some sound work in defence. More than once he has saved what appeared to be certain tries." Despite the last-gasp misses against Hunslet and Rochdale, it was the kicking that really made him stand out.

The Keighley goals record for a season stood at the 111 landed by New Zealander Joe Phillips, a former Bradford Northern full-back, in 1957–58, though it was later to be amended to 106 when five kicked in a pre-season Lazenby Cup match were removed. Garfield, who played in 35 of the 36 matches, smashed both totals easily, extending the record to 123. "Congratulations to Garry Owen on his setting up of a new club goalkicking record," ran the club programme notes for the final home match against Dewsbury. "He is really on top of his form just now and already this month he has kicked seven goals in a match on three occasions." Only 12 other Keighley players had ever done that even once since their rugby league debut season of 1900–01.

He also scored two tries, his first for Keighley coming against Liverpool City on 4 May. "Owen Try in Top Score of Season" was the headline for the match report in the *Keighley News*, which went on to say that "his first try for the club was a real gem. After dummying his way through a ruck of players he found himself clear and dashed for the line, desperately handing off defenders who were chasing him." Another try four days later against York helped bring his points total for the season to 252. Everyone thought at the time that the target to beat was Phillips's 261, which included 13 tries to add to the 111 goals, but those same amendments that deprived Garfield of the Halifax goals record, this time awarded him the Keighley points record, the figure being adjusted to 251. Not that he ever knew – by the time the change was made, Brian Jefferson had beaten both, with 155 goals and 331 points in season 1973–74. It fell to Garfield to present Jefferson with a silver salver to mark the occasion.

Operating in the Second Division had meant that Garfield was somewhat out of the limelight. The French had again asked for the Wales team to be revived, and once more it had been agreed to send a team. There were still many Welsh players around, and no need to extend the qualification rules as in the modern era. The selectors, none of whom were from Keighley and only a sprinkling from any Second Division club, did have problems finding suitable players for the hooker and prop positions, but had plenty to choose from in the backs, especially at full-back. There was to be no place for Garfield, or even Ronnie James, the choice being St Helens's Kel Coslett, who was to finish with 156 goals that season to top the lists. Coslett was yet another former rugby union international who had switched to league, having played three times for Wales in 1962. Old mate Johnny Freeman did make the team, along with Colin Dixon and Lewis Jones, and a further former union international in scrum-half Colin Evans.

If international honours were now in the past, prospects were still looking good on the club front for both Garfield and Keighley.

# 10. Time catches up

Promoted clubs in rugby league generally find life difficult in their new surroundings, and Keighley were to be no different in 1963–64, though they began with much optimism. The Eastern Region Competition was spread out over the season, enabling a proper start to be made with the league matches, the fixture compilers doing Keighley no favours by presenting them with matches at Warrington and Leeds in the first week. They were competitive at Wilderspool, losing 11–5, then triumphed against the odds at Headingley, beating Leeds 14–10, with Garfield landing four goals.

Alfred Drewry in the *Yorkshire Post* was fulsome in his praise. "Playing as though their lives depended on the result, Keighley wiped out a five-point deficit to win a furiously fast and exciting rugby league match at Headingley last night." Still in the Leeds team was Lewis Jones, who kicked magnificently, Garfield again showing his sense of sportsmanship by repeatedly applauding his artistry. Yet his own kicking was even better. "Owen landed a penalty goal from 45 yards against the wind, and others from half-way and from the touchline," wrote Drewry.

Stand-off Roy Sabine was in sparkling form in early season and won county honours for Yorkshire against Cumberland in September. However, there then followed 18 consecutive league defeats, fortunately interspersed with a 12–11 Eastern Region win over Hull KR on 26 October to prevent what would have been the worst run of defeats in the club's history. It had quickly become apparent that a side increasingly handicapped by a string of injuries, notably including Sabine whose back injury kept him sidelined for all but six early games, could not match the top teams.

Garfield played in the first 23 matches, only to then suffer injury himself, when a twisted ankle just before half-time at St Helens forced a trip to hospital. Though it proved nothing too serious, it handicapped him for more than a month. After a week's absence he tried a comeback against Oldham in the Challenge Cup at Lawkholme Lane. He succeeded with two penalties, but missed three others as a late rally made only a slight dent in the 11–2 half-time score. Keighley went out 11–4. But the ankle was still not right. He missed two further games; former Shaw Cross junior Peter Frain standing in for him.

By leap-year day, 29 February, Keighley were still without a home league victory. In town were Leeds, not in 1964 the force they often were, though they had been victors at St Helens the previous week. The match was closely contested, but with 15 minutes to go Garfield was able to put his side ahead with a penalty, and repeat the dose

Keighley 1963–64. Back: Dave Worthy, Barry Anderson, Geoff Crewdson, Syd Phillips, Albert Eyre, Mel Smith, Brian Todd; front: Ken Pye, Alf Barron, Garfield Owen, Roy Sabine, Malcolm Sharp, Gerry Jackson.

soon afterwards. Suddenly the season's tribulations were set aside, two further converted tries bringing a spectacular and very welcome final score of 22–9. A mini-revival saw a double over fellow-promoted rivals Hunslet, and a 13–7 triumph over Halifax.

Keighley had met Halifax five times that season, twice in the league, twice in the Eastern Region Competition, and once in the Yorkshire Cup. Halifax had gone on to win those last two competitions as they assembled a strong team again, built on a pack that included international Ken Roberts, Terry Fogerty and Charlie Renilson. Garfield never regretted his move to Lawkholme Lane, but did reflect on how many goals he might have kicked behind the Halifax side of the mid-1960s. As it was he recorded 78 for Keighley, who had crossed for only 50 tries. One of the 50 was scored by Garfield at Featherstone; prop Brian Gaines had been brought down inches from the line, but "at the play the ball Owen was up in support and he found the gap to score," reported the *Keighley News*. It was to be his last ever try.

Keighley avoided the wooden spoon – Hull finished two points behind them – and also avoided relegation when the two-division system was scrapped ahead of schedule. The decision had been made in February, easing the pressure in the second half of the season. Support from the Keighley public had declined, though higher numbers of visiting fans ensured the average attendance fell only slightly to just below 2,700, and gate receipts actually increased. Crowds for the Second Division clubs had been very poor, especially in the lower reaches, culminating in Keighley's neighbours Bradford Northern dropping out of the league in December after reporting losses of £400 per week. When their players were made free agents, two of them joined Keighley, South African utility player Enslin Dlambulo and prop John Hardcastle, a former Welsh schoolboy and youth rugby union international previously with Maesteg. They were followed soon afterwards by full-back Tony Beevers.

The RFL Council vote to return to one division for 1964–65 had been an emphatic 23–4, John Smallwood being with the majority. He was happier competing with all the Yorkshire clubs. "How can clubs exist without the big boys?" he asked in the press. By the time the changes were effected, a new Bradford Northern had been formed, Hardcastle returning to their ranks.

Garfield had contemplated retirement during the difficult season, because when he had first joined he had thought it likely he would remain for two years. That would have presented a problem to the club, as the local sports paper reported: "Things are going to be rather bleak for Keighley if Owen retires at the end of the season – as rumour has it he will. For the club have no ready-made successor." Work commitments were also now increasing, the job at Hoffman's Garage often entailing Saturday morning work before the Saturday afternoon match. On one occasion he travelled in the morning to Harrogate to meet a potential customer for a Rolls-Royce previously owned by one of Halifax's Mackintosh family. Finding the deal delayed and the meeting time for the match at home to Swinton looming, he quickly drove to Lawkholme Lane in the Roller, arriving at the same time as the Swinton team bus. The players seemed suitably impressed.

"Want to buy a car?" he shouted across to fellow-Welshmen Ron Morgan and Graham Rees. "You can have this one for £1,500."

"Sorry," replied Morgan. "I haven't collected this week's winning pay packet yet!"

Plans changed at the end of the season when coach Gordon Brown left, and Garfield was honoured to be asked to take over as player-coach. For Keighley it had been a difficult season, but Garfield himself had played quite well. "Keighley might be in the doldrums," ran the local press summary, "but one man whose stature has grown up in these dark Lawkholme days is Garfield Owen. It is not so much that 'Owen goal' has been the only Keighley scoreline, but that the intelligence of the genial Welshman has shone like a beacon. His touch-finding is immaculate, he fields the ball at all angles, and he has saved innumerable tries by sound defence." He could clearly manage another season.

Garfield's teaching background and playing pedigree made him an obvious choice as coach. During his captaincy he had always taken a leadership role, encouraging the younger players on the field and making efforts to inculcate good habits off it. One particular player always turned up for training straight from work in a filthy condition, and Garfield tried to persuade him to clean himself up. He was unsuccessful one time though. "If you think I'm rough," the player retorted, "you should see my wife!"

The kicking in general play was often the province of Roy Sabine, but in one match at Wigan the kicks were all in the direction of dangerman Billy Boston. Garfield pulled Sabine to one side as they left the field at half-time, suggesting he direct them instead at Eric Ashton and Frank Carlton. "We can tackle those two much more easily," he said. A Lancastrian voice piped up, saying "That's a good point!" Great Britain captain Ashton had been just behind him.

Remembering his experiences at Halifax, he said he would only accept the coaching role on the proviso that he had control of team selection. The Keighley board of directors had already conceded ground on this to Gordon Brown and 'A' team coach Joe Flanagan, so were happy to accept. Agreement was reached on a significant extra payment and the deal was struck. "Congratulations to Garry Owen on his appointment as player-coach," announced the club programme for the opening Lazenby Cup friendly encounter with Bramley. "Garry has had a couple of great seasons with us and we are looking forward to seeing how his tactics work. Garry is popular with players and spectators alike and his experience should prove him in good stead."

Garfield himself was full of expectation. "I did intend to finish at the end of last season," he admitted to the *Halifax Courier*. "I was more interested in coaching only, but I will be captain and coach next season." Flanagan, a former Keighley player and subsequent member of the club's Hall of Fame, stayed on as 'A' team coach to provide him with all the information he needed about the reserves.

In the 1960s it was not necessary to have formal qualifications for coaching, nor to have passed courses. Bill Fallowfield had begun a system, but it was not until 1974 that the National Coaching Scheme was set up under Laurie Gant and Albert Fearnley. For Garfield it was a matter of using the knowledge he had gained from his own coaches, tweaked with a few of his own ideas. There had been no coaches as such in his union days, but in league he had played under Dolly Dawson, Gareth Price, Griff Jenkins and Gordon Brown. All were trainers more than coaches in the modern sense, concentrating on getting their players fit and trying to motivate them on match days.

Halifax had been renowned for moves based around the scrum, but in a mirror of what had happened in union, these had been devised by the players involved – Stan Kielty, Ken Dean and Ken Traill primarily – while the coach worked on physical fitness exercises, interspersed with endless running up and down or lapping the pitch. There was no video footage with which to study the opposition, and little in the way of a specific game plan.

Garfield's own coaching philosophy was also based on fitness, of which he had long been both advocate and practitioner. He had always enjoyed playing the game, the enjoyment coming from being fit and properly prepared – not so much bulging muscles, but stamina and skill development, which would bring confidence and proficiency. Winning was crucial, but he wanted it to be in the best possible manner, with pride in personal appearance, smartness at training and on the field of play. Off the field, he wanted good habits like the avoidance of poor food, late nights, smoking and excessive drinking. At Keighley, his Tuesday and Thursday evening training sessions would be 90 per cent fitness work, with a short spell working on moves at the end. The players were expected to take care of the skills themselves, as he had always done, but he had plenty of advice to pass on, to both the team and individual players.

Although in control of team selection, he was not in charge of recruitment. There was no transfer activity in the summer other than the signing of a junior, 19-year-old Dave Wilmot, a Yorkshire county centre from the Shaw Cross amateur club in Dewsbury. The squad he inherited was not a big one, so there was a need for youngsters like Wilmot to be brought in; often before they were ready. Many of the others were at the opposite end of the age range, but Garfield felt he still had plenty of good players if they put their minds to it, and set firm structures in place for that to be achieved. He made it clear that players who were not at training would not be considered for selection. "Player-coach Owen seems to be the man to dictate the discipline lacking hitherto," wrote Eric Lund in *Yorkshire Sports*.

If there was a game plan of sorts, it revolved around a fit-again Roy Sabine and forward Geoff Crewdson, who could break the line and offload the ball and was later to be selected for the 1966 Great Britain Lions tour. Garfield naturally also encouraged a kicking game, but if he harboured hopes of transforming his team, they were quickly shattered. Doncaster were beaten 22–3 in the first round of the Yorkshire Cup, the only cup match of any description that Keighley ever won in his time at the club, but defeat followed at Headingley against Leeds in the second round. The league was back to its one-division format with teams meeting mostly those from their own county, and an expanded top-16 play-off at the end of the season. A defeat at Widnes was followed by home setbacks against Barrow and Leeds. There was a great 7–3 win over title-challenging outfit Wakefield Trinity in October, watched from the stands by a Welsh rugby union centre from Garfield's old stomping ground Maesteg, Les

Thomas, who was impressed enough to sign for "a great deal of money" according to the club's announcement.

Equally impressive was a derby success against the new Bradford Northern in December – "Northern Fail Against Owen" screamed the local headlines as his five goals made up the Keighley part of the 10–8 scoreline – but the play-offs were soon out of sight. Motivating the players became difficult. He would buy a round in the bar after the game when they won, but there was no danger of it bankrupting him.

By January some of the players were becoming disgruntled with the lack of winning pay. First Geoff Crewdson then hooker Barry Anderson asked to be placed on the transfer list, followed a few weeks further down the line by Roy Sabine and prop Dave Worthy. Sabine's written transfer application made clear the reasoning of them all. "I have no quarrel with the coach, any of the players, nor the directors. I feel I could do better elsewhere." Winger Mel Smith went a stage further and decided to quit the game.

Keighley needed to enter the transfer market, coincidentally targeting Garfield's former Carnegie and Halifax colleague Bryn Jones, who had lost his place in the Bradford Northern team. Jones had been one of several signings from Halifax when Bradford reformed in 1964, but Northern had now also recruited international scrum-half Tommy Smales. Jones agreed to the move and an exchange deal was arranged, Mel Smith travelling in the opposite direction.

No clubs came in for any of the transfer-listed players, so they continued at Keighley, but there was no improvement in form. York were beaten on 9 January, Garfield kicking the quickest goal of his career when York centre Houlden erred at the kick-off and he was able to land the penalty from the halfway line, but the attendance was less than 400, the lowest since the war. There was winning pay for the directors to find on gate receipts of just £63 and they quickly became as disillusioned as the players. In March, six of the nine-man board resigned, including longstanding chairman John Smallwood and that season's Yorkshire president Reg Hartley. It left just Norman Mitchell, who took over Smallwood's position, Geoff Beadnall, who had recruited most of the current players, and Supporters' Club representative Charles Redman. Again there was no fall-out, Smallwood indeed being elected as president later in the summer. They had just had enough, though they would have been aware of the club's deteriorating financial position, a loss of £4,519 on the season later being revealed – the worst return since the war.

Their last act before leaving was to appoint a new coach. Garfield had intimated a wish to relinquish the post at the end of the season, so they approached Harry Street, who had recently resigned as Castleford coach. Street, a former international, watched Keighley beat

Featherstone Rovers on 13 March, and finalised a two-year contract afterwards. "Under the terms of the contract he will come to live in Keighley," reported the local press. "In the meantime Garfield Owen, who has been combining the role of captain and coach, will continue in his present capacity."

Oldham were beaten at Lawkholme Lane the following week, encouraging the new board to dish out free tickets to local schools to build up the crowd for the match against Halifax on 27 March. The kick-off was switched to 5.30pm to avoid the televised Grand National horse race, and the reward was a gate of 2,350, helping to swell the seasonal average to 1,400. The Halifax players, it was said, had plans to stop Garfield maintaining his scoring record, he being the only player in the league left who had scored in every game that season, but in fact they helped him by giving away penalties, and he almost kicked his side to victory minutes from the end when his attempt at a drop-goal, still worth two points, narrowly missed. It enabled Halifax, who were to finish the league in seventh place and storm through to win the Championship play-offs, to scrape a 9–8 victory.

In contrast, Keighley's season fell apart dramatically and completely, the last eight league matches all being lost. At Batley both teams scored two tries, but Keighley were overwhelmed 18–8. "It is rather ironical," mused the local press report, "that Keighley who have been served magnificently by Owen's goal-kicking this season, should in effect be beaten by kicking." They finished 27th of the 30 clubs. The newspaper's end-of-season synopsis recorded that "Player-coach Garfield Owen did not have a happy start to the season with a heavy injury list complicating team selection, but despite his own fine form on the field, he never seemed able to provide the drive and planning to get the side moving with purpose. It has certainly been a memorable season for the Welsh full-back. He became the first Keighley player to obtain a century of goals twice, and the first to kick all the goals obtained by the club in a season."

In fact, the season was not completely over, for it ended with a Bottom 14 competition, which would have won any award for the silliest and least inspiring title in sporting history. It was contested under an experimental rule that allowed only one play-the-ball without interference; on the second tackle the ball had to be released, to be played by the hand or foot of any player who was standing. The rugby league lawmakers had long been vexed by the play-the-ball, for it was theoretically possible to retain possession for long periods, but were destined not to solve it until the limited-tackle rule some years later.

Most clubs did not take the Bottom 14 competition seriously, including Keighley. They were scheduled to travel to Knotty Ash to play Liverpool City in the first round, but when City became one of four teams to withdraw, they were given a walkover. Blackpool Borough were the visitors for the second round on Wednesday 5 May, a fortnight after the end of the league campaign. Harry Street took charge for the first time, with a team including eight reserves.

Garfield was one of those missing. He had played in every match during the season, kicking 103 goals when his charges had scored only 47 tries, so in a way it spoilt his record, but though he might have felt more at home with the experimental rules than most, the match just did not seem important. It developed into a glorified form of touch-and-pass, sometimes even the front-rowers kicked the ball to avoid the second tackle, and the crowd of around 500 took to shouting rugby union jargon: "Heel, Keighley!" Blackpool won 24–3. Huddersfield beat Doncaster in the final, after which the competition was sensibly scrapped.

Garfield had enjoyed the coaching aspect of the game, at least initially, but the players had not responded as much as he would have liked, and some of the youngsters had not developed as he had hoped, despite two of them gaining honours. Newcomer Les Thomas and prop Brian Gaines won selection for the under-24 international against France in April, Gaines originally as travelling reserve, but called on as a non-playing substitute on the day.

John Smallwood had been added to the selection committee, now numbering just a more manageable seven. The no-train-no-play policy had been well intentioned, but had come to a head and been abandoned. "Some weeks we would have had to play with 10 men if I had stuck to it rigidly," Garfield laments. "Some of the players just didn't want to know. I was talking to the wall I think." He found himself repeating the same advice and criticisms time after time. "Don't keep playing the same tune, Garfield," they'd complain, but never changed.

Working with professionals had been a whole lot different to the kids at Haugh Shaw and Rishworth schools, who had been so willing to listen and learn. Professional coaching was not for him anymore, and he considered that perhaps it was time to revive his plans about retirement from playing as well. He had loved his rugby, and would miss it if he did pack in, but it was maybe time to concentrate on business.

The business side of things had changed. Nine months or so after joining Hoffman's he received a phone call from Jack Sutcliffe, who owned Central Garage in Horton Street, Halifax. He had previously employed another top sportsman in Willy Watson, one of the few people to have been capped by England at both association football and cricket, and who between 1954 and 1956 had been player-manager of Halifax Town Football Club, then in the Third Division of the Football League. Watson had moved on from both the football club and the town and Garfield, with his experience at Hoffman's, seemed the ideal replacement. It was a step up for Garfield, for Jack Sutcliffe had no family, presenting good career prospects if he was successful. Sutcliffe also owned another company, which used an abbreviated form of Central Garage as its name – Cengar. Working in machine tools, Cengar Universal Tool Company Ltd was based in Lister Lane.

Keighley RLFC had their new coach firmly in place, but remained reluctant to lose Garfield as a player. They retained him on the playing register, hoping that he could turn out for them when business commitments allowed. "Keighley will start the season without their full-back Garfield Owen," announced the *Keighley News* in July. "Chairman Norman Mitchell said this week that Owen would not be available for business reasons for some time, and he may have to retire. It is understood Owen has a chance of business promotion which might interfere with his playing activities."

There was also flattering interest from Leeds, where coach Roy Francis offered him the chance to help bring on the younger lads and solve his goalkicking problems. Leeds finished sixth in 1965–66, so it could have been a good move, but the business was important now. He turned it down and Leeds instead signed Bev Risman. Although Garfield had always been lucky with injuries, at the back of his mind was the thought that he could easily get crocked. Norman Mitchell regularly phoned, trying to persuade him to continue playing for Keighley, and an unexpected offer of £600 was a serious temptation.

Jack Sutcliffe was present when a call came through and discussed the situation with Garfield. Sutcliffe's offer to give him the £600 himself was enough to finally make up his mind to retire from rugby league. Keighley fared a little better in 1965–66, moving up to 19th place in the league, but remained in its lower reaches for some time.

Garfield had played 127 matches for Keighley in his three and a half seasons, missing just five in all that time. He had amassed 703 points, only the third Keighley player to pass 700 after Joe Sherburn in the 1930s and Terry Hollindrake in the 1950s. His 348 goals was a new Keighley record, passing the total set by Hollindrake, who had kicked 320 during his nine years at the club. In those same three and a half seasons, Keighley had scored just 232 tries. In his 127 matches, he had registered goals in 115, on 25 occasions the only scores of the game for his side.

In his time at Halifax he had amassed 535 goals in 166 matches, failing to score only five times. Most seasons he had been well-placed in the game's goalkicking charts, often published in the press, his best finish being in season 1960–61 when his 130 for Keighley resulted in second place behind Austin Rhodes of St Helens. Twice he was fifth, in

1959–60 at Halifax, and in 1962–63 with Keighley. His successor at Halifax, Ronnie James, has no doubts about his skills in this respect. "He was a better goal-kicker than me," he admits. "It was spot on."

All this was in a period when goals were far harder to kick than today, though to be fair he benefited from the fact that the ball used in the 1950s and 1960s was slightly smaller than that of pre-war days. There were no artificial tees and the balls were still heavier than now, especially in wet conditions. Their inflation was also inconsistent; he eventually acquired a gauge so that for home matches he could ensure it was correct. When playing on opposition grounds he would make a nuisance of himself by trying to test the match balls before kick-off, complaining if there was anything amiss. Sometimes it had an effect, although often he was sent packing.

Only two players in the history of the game to that point had kicked goals in every match in a season, full-backs Jimmy Hoey of Widnes in 1932–33, and Billy Langton of Hunslet in 1958–59. Garfield almost managed it twice.

In the just-completed 1964–65 he had played and scored in the first 33 matches, but then missed out in 15–0 defeat against Bradford Northern in the Odsal mud on a Wednesday evening in mid-April. His solitary attempt at goal from 45 yards had direction, but fell short. "The ball was light," he remembers, "and I couldn't get any length to the kick." Bradford were able to keep Keighley far enough away from their line to make any further shot pointless.

"It was not his fault that his record went," reported the *Keighley News*. "He had a good game defensively and his touch-kicking was faultless, but his colleagues were never in enemy territory long enough to let Northern concede penalty kicks." He then failed to score again three days later, when Keighley slipped up 24–0 at Featherstone. Until then, including the final eight games of the previous season, he had actually scored in 41 consecutive matches spanning over 12 months. Five years earlier at Halifax he had scored in 43 of the 44 matches, the fly in the ointment being in a 6–6 draw at Batley on 9 January. With rule changes and a growing number of tries, the feat has been achieved many times since. The other records have now gone as well – first to Brian Jefferson with 155 goals (including 34 drop-goals) and 331 points in 1973–74. Later, in 1992–93, Keighley ran up some hefty scores in the Third Division; John Wasyliw, a former Halifax rugby union winger, racked up 187 goals and 490 points. Different times, different rules, different game.

Looking back on his career, Garfield had played consistently throughout. His success seemed greater in rugby union, where he was always with teams at the height of their game. That was not the case in his league career. Had he arrived at Halifax five years sooner he

114

would have been able to achieve so much more – there are far greater opportunities when playing in a leading side. "Sometimes the opposition seemed more dangerous when we had the ball, as we were always giving it away," he sighs. Yet he was still able to break records and win individual awards at both Halifax and Keighley.

His great achievements were saluted later by induction into the Halifax Rugby League Club's Hall of Fame. Such Halls of Fame commemorate outstanding talent and generally length of service. The latter is a stumbling block for admission to similar honours in Wales and Keighley, where his exploits were every bit as good. In the Halifax Hall of Fame he joined fellow Welshmen Jack Beames, Dai Rees, Arthur Bassett, Arthur Daniels, John Thorley, Johnny Freeman, Colin Dixon and his old adversary Ronnie James. The complete list of 38 also includes former team-mates Ken Dean, Stan Kielty, Jack Wilkinson, Alvin Ackerley, Terry Fogerty, John Burnett, Jack Scroby and Charlie Renilson. The induction came at a dinner of the Halifax Past Players' Association, when he was least expecting it. "I couldn't believe my ears," he said. "I didn't have a clue about it. It's a good job I turned up." The citation, detailing his great achievements with Halifax, was read by Brian Smith, a member of the Players' Association committee whose career had been with York and Bradford Northern rather than his home-town Halifax. Brian had known Garfield since their student days, for when Garfield was at Shoreditch, Brian was at nearby St Mary's at Strawberry Hill, great rivals on the college rugby circuit. St Mary's was a Roman Catholic establishment, but Garfield's memory was of abundant profanity and tough play on the field.

There is recognition in Wales too, where his name is engraved on the honours board at the Millennium Stadium, as the 605th player to be capped by Wales in rugby union. He was indeed to return to rugby union a few years later, and to continue his fledgling coaching career, when he was invited by Harry Wolstenholme to work with Old Crossleyans RUFC in 1973.

The town of Halifax has long been a bastion of amateur rugby, of both codes. In the 1970s, Ovenden, Illingworth, Siddal, Greetland, St Mary's and Mixenden held sway in open age rugby league, but there were just as many playing union, at Halifax RUFC, Old Brodleians, Old Rishworthians, Halifax Vandals, Heath Old Boys and Old Crossleyans. The latter, originally a club for old boys of Crossley and Porter Grammar School, had for many years been trained and coached by Stanley Sparkes, a former Pontypool player who had signed for Halifax Rugby League Club in 1931. The Rugby Football Union would not have taken kindly to the involvement of a former league player, but in Halifax a blind eye was usually turned, the two sports often working alongside each other without animosity.

During the 1950s the training facilities at Old Crossleyans had been made available to Halifax RLFC when the weather was too bad to use Thrum Hall, officials such as Harry Wolstenholme becoming popular with many of the players. So when age finally caught up with Stanley Sparkes, Garfield's similar background made him the perfect replacement as coach.

For a couple of years he was able to pass on his knowledge and experience of rugby union, providing him with both enjoyment and useful income at the same time. In Paul Beck the team had a kicker able to match his standards, and quality players like Graham Thomas and Derek Ainley who could help him ensure the improvements in the club's standing were continued. Some might have temporarily hated him when he sent them on runs on the hill they nicknamed 'Owen's Hill' behind the ground at Broomfield, down to New Lane and the woods, but they were good times, even if running the touchline in the pouring rain on a Saturday afternoon did make him question his sanity.

Although his involvement had never before been questioned, a problem arose after one victory, when the opposing club lodged a complaint about his rugby league background. By this time Paul Jackson had become a key player and influential figure. Rather than let anyone get into trouble, or the club's amateur status be challenged, it seemed best for Jackson to slip into his coaching role. Garfield's coaching tips instead became the prerogative of his son Russell, a scrum-half at school and in years to come with Old Rishworthians.

Induction into the Halifax RLFC Hall of Fame – Ken Dean does the honours.

Once rivals, soon friends. Garfield with Ronnie James at the opening of the Halifax RLFC Hall of Fame in 1993.

Press coverage over the years of a great career.

# 11. Parkinson's

Garfield and Marlene made an early decision to stay in Halifax when his rugby career ended, as many players had done before and did in the future. The likes of John Thorley and Les Pearce in the 1950s, and Colin Dixon and Ronnie James later, all made Halifax their home.

Halifax had been a great place to live. It had given them a fabulous welcome, provided them with rewarding jobs, and offered first-class educational facilities for the children. Russell and Sally were growing up and were an important consideration in the decision to stay; it would have been silly to disturb them. Both were to finish their education with excellent results, Sally at Sowerby Bridge Grammar School and Russell on a scholarship at Rishworth.

There were many friends in the town as well. Garfield's upbringing in rugby union, his business life, his involvement in golf and his appearances with Halifax Nomads cricket team, were all leading him in the same direction. In 1972 he also joined the Albany Club, a gentlemen's social club based at Hope Hall on Clare Road, where he eventually became president in 2002. "Garfield is a gentleman," remarks Halifax RLFC legend Ken Dean, "both off the field and on. A lot of the players were harsh, nasty sometimes in the heat of battle, but Garfield was different." Lots of others picked the word "gentleman" to describe him, John Burnett adding that he was simply "the nicest man I've ever met in my life."

Retirement from rugby meant there was more time for golf, the new love of his sporting career. "Golf is very much like goalkicking," wrote Gus Risman, "for as well as keeping your eye on the ball you must have perfect balance" and "the follow-through after striking the ball is immensely important." Having joined Bradley Hall back in 1957, he was taken under the wing of a good local golfer, Eric Hulme, a postman, to whom he will always be grateful, and began with a handicap of 18, the maximum in those days. He soon got a player's card and the handicap became 15. Regular practice in the morning before setting out for a day's teaching reduced his handicap to 11 and eventually three, though he saw himself as a flair player rather than a really good one.

There had been disqualifications as he became familiar with the rules. He had to forfeit the first competition he entered when he illegally practised his putting on the 18th green rather than the nearby, but busy, putting green. He was spotted by club professional Ronnie Weldon. "I'm sorry to have to tell you," he said, "but you've just disqualified yourself. You're ascertaining the speed of the greens." On another occasion there was trouble with a dog, as the *Halifax Courier* reported: "Halifax Rugby League full-back Garfield Owen had the Halifax, Huddersfield and District Golf Union officials thumbing their rule books when he returned his second round card in the handicap team competition at Dewsbury. Owen, a 14-handicap Bradley Hall member, reported that his tee shot from the 11th had landed on the fairway, where a corgi was having a romp in the sun. As Owen and his partner approached, the dog ran off, and the ball disappeared too. Obviously the dog had the ball. But the rules covering such out-of-the ordinary incidents don't allow golfers to make two and two into four."

Instead of going back to the tee and playing another ball, he continued from the point at which he estimated his original drive had finished, imposing a two-stroke penalty on himself. The committee was not impressed. They discussed first whether to impose a further two-stroke penalty for a breach of the rule, but then decided he should be disqualified completely. "If the corgi had not been in the vicinity when Garfield played the hole," suggested the *Courier* reporter, "he would probably have had a round of 66."

Teething problems overcome, he won Bradley Hall's gentlemen's stroke play competition, the John Hamer Rosebowl, for which his name was engraved on the clubhouse honours boards. It was to be the only time it would appear, because in the main competition, the Turner Trophy knockout competition, he always eventually came up against Philip Pitchforth, who was to win it eight times. Garfield was five times runner-up, but there was no recognition on the boards for that. "I thought you were a good golfer," friends teased him when scanning them. "Where's your name?" He did win the Remembrance Cup once though, when he went round in a one-below-par score of 70. With a handicap of seven, this gave him a net score of 63, enough to win by six strokes. The handicap was quickly reduced to four.

Alongside partner Philip Pitchforth he also reached the final of the Yorkshire Union foursomes tournament at Moortown in 1970. The pair beat Moortown, West End, Alwoodly, Halifax and Leeds Cobble Hall, to reach the final against Selby at Moortown. If they had won it would have been the first time one of the county's major competitions or championships had been credited to Bradley Hall, but they were beaten 8 and 7. "I played so badly. I was ashamed of myself," he regrets. The Bradley Hall centenary book is far more complimentary. "Beaten in the final by Selby in the shape of county player Les Walker and his partner Peter Huddleston," it records, "theirs was, nevertheless, a superb achievement."

In 1982 he became Halifax Golf Scratch Champion, with rounds of 70 in the morning and 76 in the afternoon, on his home course at Bradley Hall. "The Halifax area could hardly have a more popular champion," announced Jeremy Walker in the *Halifax Courier*. In a thrilling finish, he was two shots behind Halifax's Yorkshire county player John Crawshaw with two holes to play, but won both those holes to level, winning on a better back nine scores. "You have got to keep going because you never know what will happen," he told the *Courier*. "The holes you played are behind you and there is nothing you can do about it. You must look forward and keep plugging away." It was the same philosophy he applied to his goal-kicking.

In 1966 he had been asked to consider taking on the captaincy at Bradley Hall; it was a time-consuming role, but he accepted and enjoyed it. "Being captain, you meet so many people," he recollects. "You need a good memory for jokes, and need to watch your weight with all the dinners." During his year, Lord Mexborough, the owner of the land on which the course stood, was invited along to take part in a special billiards match, His Lordship being the president of the England Billiards' Association and a renowned participant. As captain, Garfield was his opponent, calling on his old skills learnt in Llanharan to beat him in a closely fought encounter. He was later greens chairman for a couple of years and president there in 1989, having been president of the Halifax, Huddersfield and District Union of Golf Clubs in 1982. It all helped to build up contacts, so important for any go-ahead businessman.

Garfield, alongside colleagues Gordon Wilkinson and Jim Patrick, became a more and more important cog in the Central Garage works during the years following the death of Jack Sutcliffe, eventually becoming sales director. In Gordon and Jim he could not have chosen two better colleagues, both having lengthy service, combined with skills he had yet to learn. Working together as a team, founded on mutual trust, they were able to make tremendous progress.

During the 1980s, Central Garage decided to sponsor a car for Halifax RLFC's Australian player-coach Chris Anderson, in return for an advertising board at the ground and a hospitality package for their chosen guests at selected matches. Halifax, whose commercial manager was Garfield's former playing colleague John Burnett, had once more become a major power in rugby league circles, winning the championship in 1986 and the Challenge Cup in 1987, and were always on the lookout for cars to bolster their deals with top players.

Fellow Australians Graham Eadie and Geoff Robinson used the car as well as Anderson, but did not treat it especially well, and did not respond to Garfield's suggestion that they bring it in to the garage on Fridays for a wash. When Anderson left, the sponsorship deal came to an end and the car was sold. "We didn't get very much for it," he remembers.

He continued his involvement with the club though, having long been a member of the Past Players' Association. He joined the

121

committee alongside such as Ken Dean, Geoff Palmer, Joe Mageen and Hubert Lockwood, becoming vice-chairman in 1990, then taking over from Jim Graydon as chairman in 1992.

Central Garage sold Simca cars when Garfield first started there, but for many years was tied to General Motors, dealing with Vauxhall cars, ahead of a later move to the South Korean-made Kia Pride cars under franchise. The economic situation in the Far East by the late 1990s was a problem, with a shortage of new cars causing trading difficulties. The garage at one point seemed likely to be swallowed up by the planned Westgate shopping centre, which would have brought a payout and relocation, but that scheme fell through in early 1998. There were other circumstances into the bargain, and eventually a decision was reached that the garage would not continue, the *Halifax Courier* reporting on 8 December 1998 that the 70-year-old dealership would close on 23 December with the loss of eight jobs. "Garage director Mr Garfield Owen said it had been a difficult decision to put the business into voluntary liquidation," wrote Michael Peel. "To have carried on in the present circumstances could have placed the company in jeopardy."

Garfield moved across to sister-company Cengar Universal Tool Company Limited, where he was already involved, in a similar sales director role. Cengar had recently designed and patented the twin-piston air-reciprocating saw, for cutting metal, plastic and timber in a wide range of industries. The saw sold so successfully that the company name became the generic term for any reciprocating saw. It was difficult for him at first, but less so as the business flourished.

The pneumatic saw's strength was that it did not create a spark like an electric saw, and was not as heavy and expensive as a hydraulic saw, and it sold well, including to every fire brigade in the country. Others tried to copy the idea; an American who worked for Cengar took it to a company over there but, with it being too expensive to sue, Cengar were able to keep their prices at such a level that the Americans could not compete. Garfield took the saw to an exhibition in Czechoslovakia, where he was able to demonstrate it in action and allow buyers to have a go, while the competition just had theirs in a glass case. Their sales manager conceded defeat. Cengar continued to thrive, but sadly Jim Patrick died of cancer and Gordon Wilkinson indicated a desire to work less hours, so in 2001 it was agreed to sell the company. It still continues to operate on the same site, one of the few pre-war engineering firms in Halifax still manufacturing.

Garfield remained fond of both codes of rugby. As a proud Welshman, he always followed the fortunes of Wales in their international matches. The main reason he has never delved into his ancestry, he jokes, is the fear of discovering that he is English. While the rugby union authorities officially continued to put the blocks on former league players becoming involved in their game in any capacity, Garfield met no problems. He attended the WRU's dinner in honour of the New Zealand touring team at Cardiff's City Hall in the Union's 1980–81 centenary season, and was also at the Barbarians' centenary dinner at the London Hilton in 1990.

Rugby union's approach changed markedly in 1995 when the game embraced professionalism for the first time. A similar attitude 100 years earlier would have resulted in just one united game of rugby, as happened when the same issues arose in football and cricket. If that had happened Garfield, Lewis Jones and the like might have won many more caps. They might also have been joined in a potentially brilliant Welsh team by such as Billy Boston and Johnny Freeman, though no black player was to be selected until more than a quarter of a century later.

By the 1990s Garfield had started to notice that there was something wrong with his health. It is hard for him to pinpoint exactly when it started, but having done a lot of PE, he was aware of his body and knew something was not right – he should not be feeling wobbly at times and he should not be occasionally sitting as though in a dream, so he sought medical advice. His doctor was Stephen Thornber, a rugby league fan who had been the Halifax RLFC doctor in the 1980s and 1990s. He knew Garfield well, and also knew what was likely to be wrong straight away. The doctor noted that Garfield's face had become a mask, so unlike it had been before. He had Parkinson's disease.

It had probably been developing for about five years or so, but many of the symptoms of Parkinson's were not yet present. His walking and balance were still fine.

Parkinson's is a disorder of part of the brain, mainly affecting the way the brain co-ordinates the movements of the muscles in various parts of the body. Its causes are unknown, and it affects one person in every 500, meaning 120,000 people in the United Kingdom alone have it. As Garfield had found, the symptoms are hardly noticeable at first, but worsen over time, and include stiffness, slowness of movement, use of small steps when walking, speech and swallowing problems, and handwriting difficulties.

He began to notice his handwriting in particular, for it had always been magnificent. It turned into a scrawl, becoming smaller and smaller. The bank had to be informed, for Cengar's exports required 10 invoices; they could be photocopied but required individually signing, and while the first signature might be fine, the last would be unrecognisable.

Father and son. Yorkshire open Golf Championship at Hawksworth Golf Club, Bradford. Son Russell (left) caddies for his dad, while the other caddy is Fenwick Allison, the former England Rugby Union full-back, who played against Garfield at Twickenham in 1956. Fenwick's son was Garfield's opponent.

Left: Halifax golf scratch champion 1982.
Right: Garfield Owen – golfer.

124

Central Garage, Halifax – Garfield in the car with Gordon Wilkinson,
Richard Canning, Andrew Ingham and the mechanics.

With friends from the Albany Club.

Later symptoms of Parkinson's can be problems with balance and falls. The earlier symptoms worsen, and new ones begin. At present there is no cure, but as advances in treatment continue, the quality of life for people with the condition also improves, and with a regime of tablets to control things, many continue to live active and fulfilling lives. Garfield has largely been able to do this, but there are inconveniencies, not least of which that he can no longer drive. Only recently in 2010 he was invited by the Welsh Rugby Union to a dinner for former international players at the Millennium Stadium, but had to decline for a combination of travel difficulties and a fear that his unsteadiness and movement problems might cause embarrassment.

Another invitation was to an afternoon of golf for former international players at the Vale Hotel Spa and Golf Resort near Cardiff. A few years earlier Garfield would have considered that to have been heaven, but by then he had been forced to give up golf completely. Around 2005, not having played at Bradley Hall for some time, he changed affiliation to West End Golf Club at Norton Tower, which was nearer his home, but rounds became rare. "I went up to West End the other day," he said in 2010, "and missed the ball completely."

As an alternative he took up bowls, joining Stafford Bowling Club, winning the Pairs Cup there in 2010. The club is near his beautiful detached home in Stafford Road, where a colour photograph of him bedecked in Welsh cap and shirt adorns the dining room. There is also a Barbarians team group, and in the hallway a Newport team photograph. Rugby union clubs were often better than rugby league at producing photographs. His various shirts and medals are not on show. "I'm proud of my achievements, but even the display of pictures I'm not sure about," he says.

Garfield joined the Halifax branch of Parkinson's UK, which gave him a chance to meet others with the condition and to acquire information. They met at Elim Pentecostal Church on Hall Street once a month. There were fundraising activities to aid research work and fund the support the charity provides, but it pained Garfield to see members working so hard to organise fairs and sales, then standing there all day to raise maybe £100. It seemed like a lot of effort for little reward. He decided to get involved and help in his own way. His experiences with the Halifax Rugby League Players' Association suggested that a sportsman's dinner was an ideal way to make money, and he set about organising one. He persuaded big-name former Welsh rugby stars Lewis Jones, Billy Boston and Kel Coslett to attend and sign autographs, and Halifax Hall of Fame member Jack Scroby to be master of ceremonies. Jack's watercolour paintings went down well in an auction at the end, and a tidy sum was raised.

With Alice Mahon MP and his drawing of the Prime Minster, Tony Blair.

His initial target was £10,000 to pay for a welfare officer responsible for visiting sufferers from the disease in Calderdale. With the help of businessman and former Halifax RLFC chairman Tony Gartland, that amount was quickly reached, so he pressed on.

Alan Kellett, the former Oldham and Halifax star, had developed a fine reputation for organising dinners for charity at Elland Cricket Club, and gave the profits from two of them to Parkinson's. Garfield helped find the speakers and guests. Welsh comedian and singer Max Boyce, who rose to prominence in the 1970s with an act combining musical comedy with his passion for rugby union, came for one of them. To the other came Cliff Morgan, Garfield's team-mate from the Wales side of the 1950s, who had gone on to become a BBC rugby union commentator and later an original team captain opposite Henry Cooper on long-running BBC television quiz show *A Question of Sport*. Garfield took a lot of the credit, but felt this should really have gone to Alan Kellett. Many of his other past team-mates have been most supportive – John Henderson, a Cumbrian who as a player always demanded the respect of his opposite number, has never been absent from a function – while the St Helens Welsh contingent continue to journey across the Pennines with regularity.

In 2010 Chris Bell of B.M. Howarth Accountants organised a further dinner for him, Garfield fixing up Falklands War survivor Simon Weston OBE as the main speaker. Ticket sales, sponsorship and an auction helped raise a further £9,000 for the Halifax branch of the society. The

127

whole business community in Halifax continued to back him, people like John Leach, Ken Davidson, Peter Lister, David Hoyle, Les Lawson, Howard Moore, Chris Hodgson, John Whittaker, Richard Blackburn and Ian Firth. "All the people of Halifax have done me proud," he says gratefully.

The auctions at dinners developed into auctions at Bonhams. Through mutual acquaintances, Garfield was able to make contact in America with Tim Shanahan, an agent for three-time world heavyweight boxing champion Muhammad Ali, himself a victim of Parkinson's. As a result he received a large number of signed items, including a boxing glove on which Ali had also written, "Service to others is the rent that we pay on earth for our room in heaven". The sale generated some £3,000, the boxing glove fetching £720.

Garfield had always been good at drawing, and in the 1990s rekindled an earlier hobby of producing pencil sketches of famous people. Using photographs and press pictures as a guide, he drew the players he knew like Les Pearce, Jack Scroby and Ken Dean, and national figures such as the Prime Minister. These he framed and gave to either the people depicted or others, many of whom were kind enough to make donations to Parkinson's, further boosting his fund-raising efforts. By 2010 the total amount he had raised had passed the £75,000 mark.

With the help of his family, he has continued to lead a happy life. Marlene has been a tower of strength. "She's a star," he says. "I couldn't have done anything without her. Dear me, no. She put up with the rugby, she put up with the golf, and now she's having to put up with Parkinson's disease." The grown-up Russell and Sally are always available too. Russell, by this time chief engineer of Control Valves division with Weir Valves & Controls in Elland, is married to Lin with a daughter Sarah. Sally, a teacher at The Gleddings Preparatory School on Birdcage Lane, is married to Russell Wilkinson with a son Owen and a daughter Eleanor. "All in all, I've had a much better life than I ever thought possible," concludes Garfield.

He has always been a participant in preference to being a spectator, but still watches both union and league, mostly nowadays from the comfort of his armchair, equally enjoying such as the Wales Grand Slam in 2008 and Halifax's Championship Grand Final triumph in 2010. He has no favourite – he enjoyed playing union and, although some in Wales thought he would not, he enjoyed his rugby league too. Both games have, of course, changed considerably since he played, not necessarily in his opinion always for the better, and both he feels need a bit of a rethink.

He has his concerns about modern day rugby union, which he feels is now too much about money. "I don't know what the game is coming to," he says, "when people see fit to use blood capsules." * Some of the tackling and running concerns him, forwards appearing to want to hurt someone, while in the mauls he feels they should attach themselves before pushing. Similarly in league, ways need to be found to reduce injuries caused by the high-speed collisions. "Rules in both games should be adhered to, or there are going to be some serious injuries," he says.

Video technology has helped remove much foul play, but in his view two good sports are being spoilt by a different kind of thuggery. He feels more players warrant being sent off, and that the authorities should then back up the referees. There was no shortage of brutality in his day – "in rugby league we knew who the hard men were and we tried to sort them out first" – but dismissals and lengthy suspensions were commonplace.

Compared with the kicking to touch in his playing days, he sees some of the kicking nowadays in union as aimless. In league, it annoys him to see many penalties despatched to touch with little thought for length. In defence he would always try to rescue a kick to touch by pulling the ball back into play, so it annoys him to see the touch judge's flag raised when a kick to touch crosses the line in the air – it should only be raised when the ball hits the ground in touch. With try-scoring, he would like to see a requirement for definite downward pressure on the ball; a sliding try he feels is a form of cheating and encourages defenders to also slide in and use their knees.

Coaching is so much more a part of both games now, but he sees many technical deficiencies, such as players not holding the ball correctly. He dislikes seeing offside players not being penalised, because they have their arms in the air claiming not to be interfering with play. In rugby league he would like to see some sort of handicapping system to aid lesser-ranked teams when they are drawn against Super League teams with their higher salary caps in cup competitions – maybe 20 points start. "People are fed up seeing the same teams in the final every year."

Cricket does not escape his criticisms either. He feels the powers-that-be are making merely half-hearted attempts to cure faults like running on the wicket - penalties for transgression should be higher. International cricket he believes is being over egged, with too many matches taking place.

Sport is in his blood, and he will always follow it, whatever the rules. As the years go by, fewer and fewer people can remember how

---

* This refers to an incident in a rugby union match, when a player faked injury using a blood capsule to allow a substitution to take place.

proficient at it he was, but it gave him a good life, and made him famous for a while.

In his introduction to this book, Garfield talks about luck. And yes, there have been some lucky breaks, in his sports activities and life in general, as his story has shown. He also remembers a match against Huddersfield at Fartown when Halifax, playing against a howling wind, scored a try by the corner flag. Placing the ball for the conversion attempt, he turned to the crowd and jokingly invited them to help by blowing in the opposite direction. Somehow the kick sailed right between the posts.

But there has been a share of bad luck as well. He suffered the loss of two of his sisters – Marion died when she was aged 10, and Gwyneth when she was 16. He had to withdraw from his first international for Wales when he was injured in a freak training ground accident. He missed out on a potential 1955 British Lions tour to South Africa when his college advised him against leave of absence. He joined Halifax RLFC when they were a top club but on the wane, played for them during some comparative lean years, and left just before they hit the heights again. There was no Welsh international rugby league side during his career for him to add to his list of international honours.

And now he has Parkinson's and all the difficulties that brings. He can no longer drive or play golf.

It would be wrong to look at his career in terms of luck. It has been about far more than that. In both union and league he was clearly an outstanding player, reaching levels to which all but a very few can only dream. He was a defensive full-back of the highest order, and a goalkicker supreme. He was a natural sportsman, able to excel in just about every game he took seriously, from cricket to athletics, golf to bowls. Away from sport he has been a successful businessman and now fundraiser. He is a Welshman that Halifax is proud to have as a resident.

# Appendix 1: Playing career record

## Rugby Union

### Newport

| | App | Tries | Cons | Pens | Drop-goals | Pts |
|---|---|---|---|---|---|---|
| 1953–54 | 3 | 0 | 0 | 0 | 0 | 0 |
| 1954–55 | 24 | 0 | 17 | 10 | 0 | 64 |
| 1955–56 | 4 | 0 | 1 | 0 | 1 | 5 |
| 1956–57 | 1 | 0 | 0 | 0 | 0 | 0 |
| **Total** | **32** | **0** | **18** | **10** | **1** | **69** |

### Wales

| | App | Tries | Cons | Pens | Drop-goals | Pts |
|---|---|---|---|---|---|---|
| 1954 to 1956 | 6 | 0 | 7 | 4 | 0 | 26 |

## Rugby League

### Halifax

| | App | Tries | Goals | Points |
|---|---|---|---|---|
| 1956–57 | 31 | 0 | 91 | 182 |
| 1957–58 | 20 | 0 | 62 | 124 |
| 1958–59 | 28 | 1 | 102 | 207 |
| 1959–60 | 44 | 2 | 145 | 296 |
| 1960–61 | 41 | 1 | 130 | 263 |
| 1961–62 | 2 | 0 | 5 | 10 |
| **Total** | **166** | **4** | **535** | **1,082** |

### Keighley

| | App | Tries | Goals | Points |
|---|---|---|---|---|
| 1961–62 | 18 | 0 | 44 | 88 |
| 1962–63 | 35 | 2 | 123 | 252 |
| 1963–64 | 37 | 1 | 78 | 159 |
| 1964–65 | 37 | 0 | 103 | 206 |
| **Total** | **127** | **3** | **348** | **705** |

### Representative matches

| | App | Tries | Goals | Points |
|---|---|---|---|---|
| 1957 to 1959 | 2 | 0 | 6 | 12 |

### Halifax / Huddersfield XIII

| | App | Tries | Goals | Points |
|---|---|---|---|---|
| 1961–62 | 1 | 0 | 1 | 2 |

### All first-class Rugby League matches

| | App | Tries | Goals | Points |
|---|---|---|---|---|
| 1956 to 1965 | 296 | 7 | 890 | 1,801 |

## Appendix 2: Representative career

### Rugby Union

**Wales 21** (4t, 3c, 1p) **I**reland **3** (1p)
Saturday 12 March 1955 at Cardiff Arms Park, Wales
*Wales:* 1. G.D. Owen (Newport), (3c), 2. K.J. Jones (Newport), 3. A.G. Thomas (Cardiff), (1p), 4. G.M. Griffiths (Cardiff) (1t), 5. H. Morris (Cardiff) (1t),
6. C.I. Morgan (Bective Rangers) (1t), 7. W.R. Willis (Cardiff), 8. W.O.G. Williams (Swansea), 9. B.V. Meredith (Newport), 10. C.C. Meredith (Neath), 11. R.J. Robins (Pontypridd), 12. R.H. Williams (Llanelli), 13. L.M. Davies (Llanelli), 14. J.R.G. Stephens (Neath), 15. R.C.C. Thomas (Swansea)
*Ireland:* 15. P.J. Berkery (Lansdowne) (1p), 14. A.C. Pedlow (Queens Uni), 13. N.J. Henderson (NIFC), 12. A.J.F. O'Reilly (Old Belvedere), 11. J.T. Gaston (Dublin Uni), 10. J.W. Kyle (NIFC), 9. S.J. McDermott (London Irish),
1. P.J. O'Donoghue (Bective Rangers), 2. R. Roe (Lansdowne),
3. F.E. Anderson (NIFC), 4. M.N. Madden (Sunday's Well), 5. R.H. Thompson (Instonians), 6. M.J. Cunningham (UC Cork), 7. G.R.P. Ross (CIYMS),
8. P. Kavanagh (Wanderers)
*Referee:* A.I. Dickie (Scotland)

**France 16** (2t, 2c, 2p) Wales **11** (1t, 1c, 1p, 1d)
Saturday 26 March 1955 at Stade Colombes, Paris, France
*France:* 15. M. Vannier (RCF) (2c, 2p), 14. H. Rancoule (FC Lourdes),
13. M. Prat (FC Lourdes), 12. R. Martine (FC Lourdes), 11. J. Lepatey (SC Mazamet), 10. A. Haget (PUC), 9. G. Dufau ((RCF), 1. R. Brejassou (S Tarbes), 2. P. Labadie (A Bayonne) 3. A. Domenech (RC Vichy), 4. R. Baulon (CS Vienne), 5. B. Chevallier (AS Montferrand), 6. M. Celaya (Biarritz Ol),
7. H. Domec (FC Lourdes), 8. J. Prat (FC Lourdes).
*Wales:* 1. G.D. Owen (Newport) (1c, 1p), 2. K.J. Jones (Newport),
3. A.G. Thomas (Llanelli) (1t), 4. G.M. Griffiths (Cardiff), 5. H.T. Morris (Cardiff), 6. C.I. Morgan (Bective Rangers), 7. W.R. Willis (Cardiff),
8. W.O.G. Williams (Swansea), 9. B.V. Meredith (Newport),
10. C.C. Meredith (Neath), 11. R.J. Robins (Pontypridd),
12. R.H. Williams (Llanelli), 13. B. Sparks (Neath), 14. J.R.G. Stephens (Neath), 15. C.D. Williams (Cardiff)
*Referee:* O.B. Glasgow (Ireland)

**England 3** (p) W**ales 8** (2t 1c)
Saturday 21 January 1956 at Twickenham, London
*England:* 1. D.F. Allison (Coventry) (1p), 2. P.B. Jackson (Coventry),
3. J. Butterfield (Northampton), 4. W.P.C. Davies (Harlequins),
5. P.H. Thompson (Headingley), 6. M.J.K. Smith (Oxford Uni), 7. R.E.G. Jeeps (Northampton), 8. D.L. Sanders (Harlequins), 9. E. Evans (Sale),
10. C.R. Jacobs (Northampton), 11. R.W.D. Marques (Cambridge Uni),
12. J.D. Currie (Oxford Uni), 13. P.G.D. Robbins (Oxford Uni), 14. A. Ashcroft (Waterloo), 15. V.G. Roberts (Harlequins).

*Wales:* 1. G.D. Owen (Carnegie) (1c), 2. K.J. Jones (Newport), 3. H.P. Morgan (Newport), 4. M.C. Thomas (Newport), 5. C.L. Davies (Cardiff) (1t), 6. C.I. Morgan (Cardiff), 7. D.O. Brace (Newport), 8. W.O.G. Williams (Swansea), 9. B.V. Meredith (Newport), 10. C.C. Meredith (Neath), 11. R.H. Williams (Llanelli), 12. R.J. Robins (Pontypridd) (1t), 13. B. Sparks (Neath), 14. L.H .Jenkins (Newport), 15. R.C.C. Thomas (Swansea)
*Referee:* R. Mitchell (Ireland)

## Wales 9 (3t) Scotland 3 (1p)
Saturday 4 February 1956 at Cardiff Arms Park, Wales
*Wales:* 1. G.D. Owen (Carnegie), 2. K.J. Jones (Newport), 3. H.P. Morgan (Newport) (1t), 4. M.C. Thomas (Newport), 5. C.L. Davies (Cardiff) (1t), 6. C.I. Morgan (Cardiff) (1t), 7. D.O. Brace (Newport), 8. W.O.G. Williams (Swansea), 9. B.V. Meredith (Newport), 10. R. Prosser (Pontypool), 11. R.H. Williams (Llanelli), 12. J.R.G. Stephens (Neath), 13. B. Sparks (Neath), 14. L.H. Jenkins (Newport), 15. R.C.C. Thomas (Swansea).
*Scotland:* 1. R.W.T. Chisholm (Melrose), 2. A.R. Smith (Cambridge Uni) 3. A. Cameron (Glasgow HSFP) (1p), 4. K.R. MacDonald (Stewart's FP) 5. J.S. Swan (Coventry), 6. M.L. Grant (Harlequins), 7. N.M. Campbell (London Scottish), 8. H.F. McLeod (Hawick), 9. R.K.G. MacEwan (London Scottish), 10. T. Elliott (Gala), 11. E.J.S. Michie (Aberdeen GSFP), 12. J.W.Y. Kemp (Glasgow HSFP), 13. I.A.A. MacGregor (Llanelli), 14. J.T. Greenwood (Dunfermline), 15. A. Robson (Hawick).
*Referee:* L.M. Bound (England)

## Ireland 11 (1t, 1c, 1p, 1d) Wales 3 (1p)
Saturday 10 March 1956 at Lansdowne Road, Dublin
*Ireland:* 15. P.J. Berkery (Lansdowne), 14. S.V.J. Quinlan (Highfield), 13. N.J. Henderson (NIFC), 12. A.J.F. O'Reilly (Old Belvedere), 11. A.C. Pedlow (Queens Uni) (1c, 1p), 10. J.W. Kyle (NIFC) (1d), 9. J.A. O' Meara (Dolphin), 1. P.J. O' Donoghue (Bective Rangers), 2. R. Roe (London Irish), 3. B.G.M. Wood (Garryowen), 4. R.H. Thompson (Istonians), 5. J.R. Brady (CIYMS), 6. M.J. Cunningham (Cork Constitution) (1t), 7. T. McGrath (Garryowen), 8. J.R. Kavanagh (Wanderers).
*Wales:* 1. G.D. Owen (Carnegie) (1p), 2. K.J. Jones (Newport), 3. H.P. Morgan (Newport), 4. M.C. Thomas (Newport), 5. C.L .Davies (Cardiff), 6. C.I. Morgan (Cardiff), 7. D.O. Brace (Newport), 8. W.O.G. Williams (Swansea), 9. B.V. Meredith (Newport), 10. C.C. Meredith (Neath), 11. J.R.G. Stephens (Neath), 12. R.H. Williams (Llanelli), 13. B. Sparks (Neath), 14. L.H. Jenkins (Newport), 15. R.C.C. Thomas (Swansea).
*Referee:* A.I. Dickie (Scotland)

## Wales 5 (1t, 1c) France 3 (1t)
Saturday 24 March 1956 at Cardiff Arms Park, Wales
*Wales:* 1. G.D. Owen (Carnegie) (1c), 2. K.J. Jones (Newport), 3. H.P. Morgan (Newport), 4. M.C. Thomas (Newport), 5. G. Rowlands (Cardiff), 6. C.I. Morgan (Cardiff), 7. D.O. Brace (Newport), 8. R. Richards (Cross Keys), 9. B.V. Meredith (Newport), 10. R. Prosser (Pontypool), 11. L.H. Jenkins (Newport), 12. J.R.G. Stephens (Neath), 13. C.D. Williams (Neath) (1t),

14. R.J. Robins (Pontypridd), 15. G. Whitson (Newport).
*France:* 15. M. Vannier (RCF), 14. J. Dupuy (S Tarbes), 13. M. Prat (FC Lourdes), 12. A. Boniface (S. Mont-de-Marsan), 11. L. Roge (AS Beziers), 10. J. Bouquet (CS Vienne) (1t), 9. G. Dufau (RCF), 2. A. Domenech (CA Brive), 1. R. Vigier (AS Montferrand), 3. R. Bienes (US Cognac), 4. B. Chevallier (AS Montferrand), 5. M. Celaya (Biarritz Ol), 6. R. Baulon (A Bayonne), 7. J. Barthe (FC Lourdes), 8. H. Domec (FC Lourdes).
*Referee:* Dr P.F. Cooper (England)

## Rugby League

**Northern Rugby League XIII 19** (3t, 5g) France **8** (2t, 1g)
Wednesday 16 April 1958 at Headingley, Leeds.
*Northern Rugby League XIII:* 1. G.D. Owen (Halifax) (5g) 2. B. Bevan (Warrington) (1t), 3. K. McLellan (Leeds), 4. B.L. Jones (Leeds), 5. K.T. van Vollenhoven (St Helens) (2t), 6. B.L. Gabbitas (Hunslet), 7. J.M. Stevenson (Leeds), 8. J. Wilkinson (Halifax), 9. S. Smith (Hunslet), 10. S.G. Owen (Leigh), 11. D. Holland (Hull KR), 12. P. Norburn (Swinton), 13. E.W. Dawson (York).
*France:* 1. A. Rives (Albi) (1g), 2. R. Contrastin (Bordeaux), 3. A. Delpoux (Carcassonne), 4. A. Jiminez (Villeneuve) (1t), 5. G. Husson (Albi), 6. F. Levy (Perpignan), 7. G. Fages (Albi), 8. J.M. Bez (Albi), 9. A. Apelian (Jomville), 10. R. Lacans (Lezignan), 11. G. Verdier (Albi), 12. R. Marjoral (Perpignan), 13. J. Rouqueirol (Avignon).
Referee: M. Coates (Pudsey)
Attendance 13,993

**France 25** (5t, 5g) **Wales 8** (2t, 1g)
Sunday 1 March 1959 at Toulouse, France.
*France:* 1. A. Rives, 2. M. Voron, 3. A. Jiminez, 4. A. Carrere (1t), 5. A. Savonne (1t), 6. G. Benausse (1t, 5g), 7. B. Fabre (1t), 8. A. Boldini, 9. A. Apelian, 10. R. Lacans, 11. R. Eramouspe, 12. S. Tonus, 13. J. Rouqueirol (1t).
*Wales:* 1. G.D. Owen (Halifax) (1g), 2. L. Emmitt (Blackpool), 3. G. Lewis (Leigh), 4. J. Cheshire (Salford) (1t), 5. M. Davies (Bradford N.), 6. G. Jones (Salford) (1t), 7. R. Thomas (Wigan), 8. G.M.J. Thorley (Halifax), 9. P.T. Harris (Hull), 10. D.G. Vines (Wakefield), 11. D. Moses (Swinton), 12. G. Parsons (Salford), 13. C. Winslade (Oldham).
*Referee:* J. Queroli (Perpignan)
Attendance 25,000

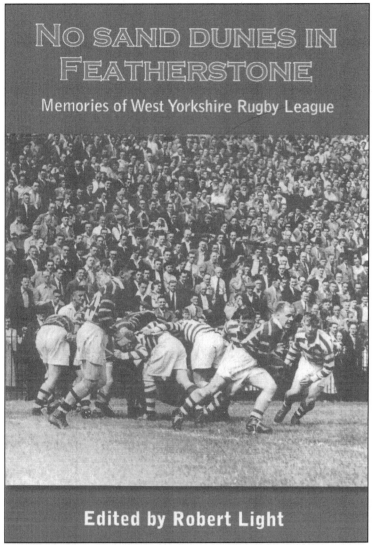

# NO SAND DUNES IN FEATHERSTONE

## Memories of West Yorkshire Rugby League

## Edited by Robert Light

Based on the *'Up and Under'* University of Huddersfield oral history project, this book includes memories from players, coaches, club officials, referees, journalists and supporters from the First World War to the present. Every rugby league supporter will enjoy this fascinating book. Published in October 2010 at £12.95. Available direct from London League Publications Ltd for just £12.00. For credit card payments visit www.llpshop.co.uk , cheque payments to PO Box 65784, London NW2 9NS, cheques payable to London League Publications Ltd. It can also be ordered from any bookshop for £12.95 (ISBN: 9781903659533).

# Braver than all the rest

## A mother fights for her son

## Philip Howard

Dave and Sarah Burgess are devastated when their young son Karl is found to have muscular dystrophy. Then another tragedy hits the family hard. But the family are committed to do the best they can for Karl, who has a passion for rugby league. Based in Castleton, a Yorkshire town near the border with Lancashire, Karl's determination to get the most out of life, despite his disability, inspires those around him, in particular Chris Anderton, one of the Castleton Rugby League Club players.

Philip Howard is a retired teacher who had responsibility for special needs at a sixth form college. He is a lifelong rugby league fan from St Helens, but now lives near Hull. This is his first novel.

Published in September 2010 at £9.95. Available direct from London League Publications Ltd for just £9.00 post free. For credit card payments visit www.llpshop.co.uk , cheque payments to PO Box 65784, London NW2 9NS, payable to London League Publications Ltd. It can also be ordered from any bookshop for £9.95 (ISBN: 9781903659526).